BUILDING TO LAST

ANDREW CARNEGIE'S

PRINCIPLES FOR

WEALTH & LEGACY

BY

ANDREW CARNEGIE

I0518336

choice
P R e S S

Choice Press LLC
15954 Jackson Creek Pkwy, Suite B,
Box 501, Monument CO, 80132

choice-press.com

Cover art by Akihiro Nakayama
Set in Georgia font
Printed in the United States of America.

ISBN 979-8-9926998-1-4

CONTENTS

FOREWORD

What's most impressive about Andrew Carnegie is how radically he differed from the typical mindset of his time. While many used wealth to showcase status or power, Carnegie saw it as a moral responsibility. He believed that the rich were not owners of their fortune, but stewards. That belief was bold and, in many ways, countercultural.

He was consistent in acting this out. He didn't just talk about philanthropy. He lived it. He funded over 2,500 libraries, supported schools, and poured resources into creating opportunities for the working class. In an age of stark economic inequality, his vision of using wealth to elevate society, not just himself, set a precedent for what it means to be a purpose-driven capitalist.

That vision resonates with my own life, and as you read this book, it will resonate with yours as well.

BUILDING TO LAST

While Carnegie gave back through traditional institutions like libraries and universities, I've tried to do something similar through the Raising Alphas Project. Our aim is to elevate our children, teaching them real-world applications drawn from entrepreneurs, business professionals, and those who have walked the walk. It's about reinvesting, through time, experience, and mentorship, into the next generation.

Like Carnegie, I believe in building wealth with a purpose. While I don't agree with every aspect of his worldview, understandably given that he lived in a very different era, I admire his drive, his discipline, and his sense of responsibility. He had a pure goal: to create wealth and use it to uplift others. That's something I try to embody in my own life, and it's why his story still matters.

Revisiting Carnegie's thoughts on money, work, and success is more relevant today than ever. His practical yet moral approach offers a sharp contrast to today's flashier, exploitative models of success. In a culture that often equates wealth with clout or personal branding, Carnegie's belief that money should serve the greater good feels almost radical. He reminds us that success isn't just about accumulation. It's about contribution. He challenges us to redefine wealth not as a symbol, but as a tool.

I've often said this: *money is a tool.*

A shovel isn't evil. It's just something to dig the ground and build something lasting with. That's how Carnegie saw money: so build something lasting with.

This book can benefit a wide range of readers, especially those not just chasing success but seeking significance. In this book, entrepreneurs will find timeless principles for building wealth with purpose, while young professionals can align their ambition with integrity. Legacy-minded families will find a framework for passing down not just assets, but timeless values.

That's something I speak about often with Raising Alphas. I want my kids to inherit more than money. I want them to understand family values, responsibility, and self-discipline. I didn't really start learning about wealth and how to grow it until my late thirties. I had the ambition, but not the roadmap. This book helps provide that roadmap.

Whether you're a seasoned professional or just starting out, Carnegie's reflections will challenge you to think deeply. They push you to ask not just, "How do I succeed?" but "How do I build something that matters?"

This modern edition of Carnegie's wisdom perfectly reflects the mission of our Choice Legacy imprint. At Choice Legacy, we preserve and modernize timeless works that emphasize ethical leadership, generational thinking, and value-based enterprise. Carnegie is a perfect model for that. His life bridges self-made entrepreneurship and large-scale public service. His legacy wasn't built on what he kept, but on what he gave. That's the heart of the Choice Legacy vision: curating voices that remind us of what matters most.

Approach this book as a manual and a mentor. Don't rush. Take your time. Read a chapter, pause, and reflect. That's why we included reflection prompts: to help you wrestle with the deeper truths here. Use this book as a conversation. Let Carnegie's words challenge your assumptions and sharpen your goals.

After closing this book, I hope that you will carry away from it a conviction, a desire to build something meaningful and enduring, not just profitable. If even one decision, one investment, or one legacy plan you make is shaped by this book, then this book has done its job. After all, like money, this book is a tool for your success.

Maybe, years from now, someone will be recording a foreword to their own book. Maybe they'll mention you, because you gave them inspiration like Andrew Carnegie gave. Maybe they'll say that your name still lives on.

If so, it's because you took the risk. You faced the giants in your life. You built something that lasted. May this book help you to build something that will last.

~Stephen Davis

INTRODUCTION

In an age when success is often measured by speed, the life of Andrew Carnegie reminds us that true wealth is built with purpose, patience, and principle. Born into poverty in Dunfermline, Scotland in 1835, Carnegie immigrated to the United States as a boy and began working in a cotton factory at the age of thirteen. Through determination, discipline, and a relentless pursuit of opportunity, he rose to become one of the wealthiest industrialists of the Gilded Age. As founder of Carnegie Steel, and later as one of the most influential philanthropists in history, he believed that wealth was not simply to be accumulated but to be used wisely for the good of others.

Carnegie was more than a businessman. He was a thinker, a builder, and a firm believer in the moral obligation of the successful to uplift others. His writing reflects this vision. First published in 1902, *The Empire of Business* collected his personal reflections on success, labor, industry, and responsibility. With this new edition, retitled *Building to Last: Andrew Carnegie's Principles for Wealth and Legacy*, we are proud to present these timeless insights to a modern readership.

This volume is published under the Choice Legacy imprint of Choice Press, where our mission is to preserve and share the wisdom of those who built lasting impact through their lives and work. *Building to Last* stands as one of many flagship titles in that effort, offering guidance that speaks across generations.

While this edition honors the original structure of Carnegie's work, some punctuation, spelling, and phrasing have been gently updated for clarity and readability. The ideas remain untouched in their strength and conviction. Readers today will find in these pages a clear and challenging vision: success that endures must be rooted in values deeper than profit.

This edition includes six of Carnegie's core essays, each shown through the lens of legacy-building:

General Introduction

1. **Lessons for the Young**

   Advice for those beginning their journey, rooted in character, initiative, and self-discipline.

2. **The A-B-C's of Money**

   Practical, enduring truths about earning and managing wealth.

3. **On the Common Interest of Labor and Capital**

   A forward-thinking call for shared purpose between worker and owner.

4. **Thrift as Duty**

   On the civic and moral power of frugality.

5. **How to Win Fortune**

   Guidance on recognizing opportunity and creating one's path.

6. **Wealth and Its Uses**

   Carnegie's defining essay on stewardship, generosity, and lasting influence.

   Each chapter is followed by an interactive section featuring guided questions and reflection prompts. These are designed to help you slow down, absorb the material, and connect Carnegie's counsel to your own life and aspirations.

We encourage you to treat this book as more than a historical document. It is a personal tool, a prompt for deeper thought, and perhaps even a spark for your own legacy. As you read, consider how your own story might be preserved. Whether through a personal memoir, a legacy journal, or meaningful conversations with your family and community, your experiences hold value and wisdom that deserve to be passed down.

At Choice Press, we believe that building something that lasts begins with reflection, intention, and the courage to share your journey. May this book inspire you to do just that.

Chapter 1

Lessons for the Young

It is well that the young should begin at the beginning and occupy the most subordinate positions. Many of the leading businessmen of Pittsburg had a serious responsibility thrust upon them at the very threshold of their career. They were introduced to the broom and spent the first hours of their business lives sweeping out the office.

I notice we have janitors and janitresses now in offices, and our young men unfortunately miss that salutary branch of a business education. But if by chance the professional sweeper is absent any morning, the boy who has the genius of the future partner in him will not hesitate to try his hand at the broom. The other day a fond fashionable mother in Michigan asked a young man whether he had ever seen a young lady sweep in a room so grandly as her Priscilla. He said no, he never had, and the mother was gratified beyond measure, but then said he, after a pause, "What I should like to see her do is sweep out a room."

It does not hurt the newest comer to sweep out the office if necessary. I was one of those sweepers myself, and who do you suppose were my fellow sweepers? David McCargo, now super-intendent of the Alleghany Valley Railroad, Robert Pitcairn, super-intendent of the Pennsylvania Railroad, and Mr. Moreland, city attorney.

We all took turns; two each morning did the sweeping. I remember Davie was so proud of his clean white shirt bosom that he used to spread over it an old silk bandana handkerchief which he kept for the purpose, and we other boys thought he was putting on airs. So he was. None of us had a silk handkerchief.

My advice to you is aim high.

I would not give a fig for the young man who does not already see himself the partner or the head of an important firm. Do not rest content for a moment in your thoughts as head clerk, or foreman, or general manager in any concern, no matter how extensive.

Say each to yourself, "My place is at the top."

Lessons for the Young

Be king in your dreams. Make your vow that you will reach that position, with untarnished reputation, and make no other vow to distract your attention, except the very commendable one that when you are a member of the firm or before that, if you have been promoted two or three times, you will form another partnership with the loveliest of her sex. The liability there is never limited.

Let me indicate **two or three conditions essential to success.** Do not be afraid that I am going to moralize or inflict a homily upon you. I speak upon the subject only from the view of a man of the world, desirous of aiding you to become successful businessmen. You all know that there is no genuine, praiseworthy success in life if you are not honest, truthful, fair dealing. I assume you are and will remain all these, and that you are determined to live pure, respectable lives, free from pernicious or equivocal associations with one sex or the other. There is no more creditable future for you else. Otherwise, your learning and your advantages not only go for naught but serve to accentuate your failure and your disgrace.

BUILDING TO LAST

I hope you will not take it amiss if I warn you against **three of the gravest dangers** which will beset you in your upward path.

The first and most seductive destroyer of young men is the drinking of **liquor**. I am no temperance lecturer in disguise, but a man who knows and tells you what observation has proved to him. You are more likely to fail in your career by acquiring the habit of drinking liquor than from any other temptations likely to assail you. You may yield to almost any other temptation, reform, and if not recover lost ground, at least remain in the race and secure and maintain a respectable position. But from the insane thirst for liquor escape is almost impossible. I know but few exceptions to this rule.

You must not drink liquor to excess. Better if you do not touch it at all. If this is too hard a rule for you then resolve never to touch it except at meals. A glass at dinner will not hinder your advance in life or lower your tone, but I implore you hold it inconsistent with the dignity and self-respect of gentlemen, with what is due from yourselves to yourselves, being the men you are, and especially the men you are determined to become, to drink a glass of liquor at a bar. Be far too much of the gentleman ever to enter a barroom. You do not pursue your careers in safety unless you stand firmly upon this ground. Adhere to it and you have escaped danger from the deadliest of your foes.

The next greatest danger to a young businessman is **speculation**. When I was a telegraph operator, we had no exchanges in the city, but the men or firms who speculated upon the Eastern Exchanges were necessarily known to the operators. They could be counted on the fingers of one hand. These men were not our citizens of first repute: they were regarded with suspicion. I have lived to see all these speculators irreparably ruined men, bankrupt in money, and bankrupt in character.

There is scarcely an instance of a man who has made a fortune by speculation and kept it. Gamesters die poorly and there is certainly not an instance of a speculator who has lived a life creditable to himself or advantageous to the community. The man who grasps the morning paper to see first how his speculative ventures upon the exchanges are likely to result, unfits himself for the calm consideration and proper solution of business problems, with which he has to deal later in the day, and saps the sources of that persistent and concentrated energy upon which depend the permanent success, and often the very safety, of his main business.

The speculator and the businessman tread diverging lines. The former depends upon the sudden turn of fortune's wheel, a millionaire today, a bankrupt to-morrow. But the man of business knows that only by years of patient, unremitting attention to affairs can he earn his reward, which is the result, not of chance, but of well-devised means for the attainment of ends.

Say to the tempter who asks you to risk your small savings, that if ever you decide to speculate you are determined to go to a regular and well-conducted house where they cheat fairly. You can get fair play and about an equal chance upon the red and black in such a place; upon the exchange you have neither. You might as well try your luck with the three-card-monte man.

There is another point involved in speculation. Nothing is more essential to young businessmen than untarnished credit, credit begotten of confidence in their prudence, principles, and stability of character. Well, believe me, nothing kills credit sooner in any bank board than the knowledge that either firms or men engage in speculation. It matters not a whit whether gains or losses be the temporary result of these operations. The moment a man is known to speculate, his credit is impaired, and soon thereafter it is gone. How can a man be credited whose resources may be swept away in one hour by a panic among gamesters? Who can tell how he stands among them? Except that this is certain: he has given due notice that he may stand to lose all, so that those who credit him have themselves to blame.

Resolve to be businessmen, but speculators never.

The third and last danger against which I shall warn you is one which has wrecked many a fair craft which started well and gave promise of a prosperous voyage. It is the perilous habit of **endorsing** — even more dangerous, since it assails one generally in the garb of friendship. It appeals to your generous instincts, and you say, "How can I refuse to lend only my name to assist a friend?"

It is because there is so much that is true and commendable in that view that the practice is so

BUILDING TO LAST

dangerous. Let me endeavor to put you upon safe honorable grounds about it. I would say to you to make it a rule now, never endorse; but this is too much like 'never taste wine', or 'never smoke'. They generally result in exceptions. You will as businessmen now and then probably become security for friends. Now, here is the line at which regard for the success of friends should cease and regard for your own honor begins.

If you owe anything, all your capital and all your effects are a solemn trust in your hands to be held inviolate for the security of those who have trusted you. Nothing can be done by you with honor which jeopardizes these first claims upon you. When a man in debt endorses for another, it is not his own credit or his own capital he risks, it is that of his own creditors. He violates trust. Mark you then, never endorse until you have cash means not required for your own debts and never endorse beyond those means.

Before you endorse at all, consider endorsements as gifts, and ask yourselves whether you wish to make the gift for your friend and whether the money is really yours to give and not a trust for your creditors. You are not safe unless you stand firmly upon this as the only ground which an honest businessmen can occupy.

I beseech you avoid liquor, speculation and endorsement. Do not fail in either, for liquor and speculation are the Scylla and Charybdis of the young man's business sea, and endorsement his rock ahead.

Assuming you are safe regarding these gravest dangers, the question now is **how to rise from the subordinate position** we have imagined you in, through the successive grades to the position for which you are evidently intended.

I can give you the secret. It lies mainly in this. Instead of the question, "What must I do for my employer?" substitute "What can I do?"

Faithful and conscientious discharge of the duties assigned you is all very well, but the verdict in such cases generally is that you perform your present duties so well that you had better continue performing them. This will not do. It will not do for the coming partners. There must be something beyond this. We make clerks, bookkeepers, treasurers, bank tellers of this class, and there they remain to the end of the chapter. The rising man must do something exceptional, and beyond the range of his special department.

He must attract attention.

A shipping clerk may discover in an invoice an error with which he has nothing to do, and which has escaped the attention of the proper party. If a weighing clerk, he may save for the firm by doubting the adjustment of the scales and having them corrected, even if this is the province of the master mechanic. If a messenger boy, even he can lay the seed of promotion by going beyond the letter of his instructions in order to secure the desired reply. There is no service so low and simple, neither any so high, in which the young man of ability and willing disposition cannot readily and almost daily prove himself capable of greater trust and usefulness and show his invincible determination to rise.

Someday, in your own department, you will be directed to do or say something which you know will prove disadvantageous to the interest of the firm. Here is your chance. Stand up like a man and say so. Say it boldly and give your reasons and prove to your employer that, while his thoughts have been engaged upon other matters, you have been studying during hours when perhaps he thought you asleep, how to advance his interests. You may be right or you may be wrong, but in either case, you have gained the first condition of success. You have attracted attention.

Your employer has found that he has not a mere hireling in his service, but a man; not one who is content to give so many hours of work for so many dollars in return, but one who devotes his spare hours and constant thoughts to the business. Such an employe must perforce be thought of kindly and well. It will not be long before his advice is asked in his special branch, and if the advice given is sound, it will soon be asked and taken upon questions of broader bearing. This means partnership, if not with present employers, then with others. Your foot, in such a case, is upon the ladder; the amount of climbing done depends entirely upon yourself.

Always break orders to save owners. There never was a great character who did not sometimes smash the routine regulations and make new ones for himself. You are destined to be owners and to make orders and break orders. Do not hesitate to do it whenever you are sure the interests of your employer will be thereby promoted and when you are so sure of the result that you are willing to take responsibility.

You will never be a partner unless you know the business of your department far better than the owners possibly can. When called to account for your independent action, show him the result of your genius, and tell him that you knew that it would be so; show him how mistaken the orders were. Boss your boss just as soon as you can; try it on early. There is nothing he will like so well if he is the right kind of boss. If he is not, he is not the man for you to remain with, leave him whenever you can, even at a present sacrifice, and find one capable of discerning genius. Our voting partners in the Carnegie Firm have won their spurs by showing that we did not know half as well as they did. Some of them have acted upon occasion with me as if they owned the firm and I was but some airy New Yorker presuming to advise upon what I knew very little about. Well, they are not interfered with much now. They were the true bosses, the very men we were looking for.

There is one sure mark of the future millionaire. His revenues always exceed his expenditures. He begins to save early, almost as soon as he begins to earn. No matter how little it may be possible to save, save that little. Invest it securely, not necessarily in bonds, but in anything which you have good reason to believe will be profitable, but no gambling with it, remember. A rare chance will soon present itself for investment. The little you have saved will prove the basis for an amount of credit utterly surprising to you. Capitalists trust the saving young man. For every hundred dollars you can produce as the result of hard-won savings, Midas, in search of a partner, will lend or credit a thousand; for every thousand, fifty thousand. It is not capital that your seniors require, it is the man who has proved that he has the business habits which create capital, and to create it in the best of all possible ways, as far as self-discipline is concerned, is, by adjusting his habits to his means.

It is the first hundred dollars saved which tells. Begin at once to lay up something. The bee predominates in the future millionaire.

Of course there are better, higher aims than saving. As an end, the acquisition of wealth is ignoble in the extreme. I assume that you save and long for wealth only as a means of enabling you the better to do some good in your day and generation. Make a note of this essential rule: **Expenditure always within income.**

You may grow impatient or become discouraged when year by year you float on in subordinate positions. There is no doubt that it is becoming harder and harder as business gravitates more and more to immense concerns, for a young man without capital to get a start for himself, and where large capital is essential, it is unusually difficult.

Still, let me tell you for your encouragement that there is no country in the world where able and energetic young men can so readily rise as the United States. It has been impossible to meet the demand for capable, first-class bookkeepers. The supply has never been equal to the demand. Young men give all kinds of reasons why in their cases failure was clearly attributable to exceptional circumstances which render success impossible. Some never had a chance, according to their own story.

This is simply nonsense. No young man ever lived who had not a chance, and a splendid chance, too, if he ever was employed at all. He is assayed in the mind of his immediate superior, from the day he begins work, and, after a time, if he has merit, he is assayed in the council chamber of the firm. His ability, honesty, habits, associations, temper, disposition, all these are weighed and analyzed. The young man who never had a chance is the same young man who has been canvassed repeatedly by his superiors and found destitute of necessary qualifications, or is deemed unworthy of closer relations with the firm, owing to some objectionable act, habit, or association, of which he thought his employers ignorant.

Another class of young men attribute their failure to employers having relations or favorites whom they advanced unfairly. They also insist that their employers disliked brighter intelligences than their own, and were disposed to discourage aspiring genius, and delighted in keeping young men down. There is nothing in this.

On the contrary, there is no one suffering so much for lack of the right man in the right place, nor so anxious to find him as the owner. There is not a firm today which is not in constant search for business ability, and every one of them will tell you that there is no article in the market at all times so scarce. **There is always a boom in brains**. Cultivate that crop, for if you grow any amount of that commodity, here is your best market and you cannot overstock it, and the more brains you have to sell, the higher price you can exact. They are not quite so sure a crop as wild oats, which never fail to produce a bountiful harvest, but they have the advantage over these in always finding a market.

Do not hesitate to engage in any legitimate business, for there is no business in America, I do not care what, which will not yield a fair profit if it receives the exclusive attention and capital of capable and industrious men. Every business will have its season of depression — years always come during which the manufacturers and merchants of the city are severely tried — years when mills must be run, not for profit, but at a loss, that the organization and men may be kept together and employed, and the concern may keep its products in the market. But on the other hand, every legitimate business producing or dealing in an article which man requires is bound in time to be profitable if properly conducted.

And here is **the prime condition of success**, the great secret: concentrate your energy, thought, and capital exclusively upon the business in which you are engaged. Having begun in one line, resolve to fight it out on that line, to lead in it; adopt every improvement, have the best machinery, and know the most about it.

The concerns which fail are those which have scattered their capital, which means that they have scattered their brains also. They have investments in this, or that, or the other, here, there and everywhere. Don't put all your eggs in one basket is all wrong. Put all your eggs in one basket and then watch that basket. Look round you and take notice; men who do that do not often fail. It is easy to watch and carry the one basket. It is trying to carry too many baskets that breaks most eggs in this country. He who carries three baskets must put one on his head, which is apt to tumble and trip him up. One fault of the American businessman is his lack of concentration.

To summarize what I have said:

- Aim for the highest

- Do not touch liquor, or if at all, only at meals

- Never speculate

- Never endorse beyond your surplus cash fund

BUILDING TO LAST

- Make the firm's interest yours

- Break orders always to save owners

- Concentrate

- Put all your eggs in one basket, and watch that basket

- Expenditure always within revenue

- Be not impatient

I congratulate poor young men upon being born to that ancient and honorable degree which renders it necessary that they should devote themselves to hard work. A basketful of bonds is the heaviest basket a young man ever had to carry. He generally gets to staggering under it. We have in this city creditable instances of such young men, who have pressed to the front rank of our best and most useful citizens. These deserve great credit. But the vast majority of the sons of rich men are unable to resist the temptations to which wealth subjects them and sink to unworthy lives. I would almost as soon leave a young man a curse as burden him with the almighty dollar. It is not from this class you have rivalry to fear. The partner's sons will not trouble you much, but look out that some boys poorer, much poorer than yourselves, whose parents cannot afford to give them the advantages of a course in this institute, advantages which should give you a decided lead in the race — look out that such boys do not challenge you at the post and pass you at the grand stand.

Look out for the boy who has to plunge into work direct from the common school and who begins by sweeping out the office. He is the probable dark horse that you had better watch.

Reflection Section

Lessons for the Young

Andrew Carnegie's first lesson is clear: greatness begins in the lowliest tasks, if approached with ambition, integrity, and vision. From sweeping offices to making executive decisions, each step in a career should be grounded in character. Carnegie urges young readers to aim high, guard their reputation, and rise not by privilege, but by earning trust, showing initiative, and thinking beyond assigned duties. He identifies the greatest dangers to success—liquor, speculation, and careless endorsements—and outlines a practical philosophy of concentrated effort, consistent savings, and personal excellence.

Guided Reflection

1. **"My place is at the top."**

Lessons for the Young

Carnegie believed that aspiring to leadership is essential from the very start.

- What does "the top" look like for you in your current season of life or work?

- Have you allowed yourself to dream boldly about your future, or have you settled for smaller roles than you are capable of?

2. Begin with what's in your hand.

Even the most mundane tasks can be foundational.

- What is one "small" task you can approach with excellence and initiative this week?

- How might you exceed expectations in a way that benefits your team, client, or mission?

3. Avoid the traps.

Carnegie warns of three dangers: alcohol, speculation, and endorsing debts you can't afford.

- Have any of these (or their modern equivalents) ever threatened to derail your focus, finances, or reputation?

- What boundaries can you put in place to protect your long-term integrity?

4. Serve like an owner.

"Make the firm's interest yours," he says.

- Do you treat your current work as if it were your own company or cause?

- Where can you take initiative or voice a bold idea, even if it isn't part of your job description?

5. Invest early in yourself.

Carnegie emphasizes saving, concentration, and self-discipline as marks of the future millionaire.

- What is one habit—financial or otherwise— that you can begin now to build your foundation for legacy?

Chapter 2

The A-B-C's of Money

I suppose everyone who has spoken to or written for the public has wished at times that everybody would drop everything and just listen to him for a few minutes. I feel so this morning, for I believe that a grave injury threatens the people and the progress of our country simply because the masses, the farmers and the wage-earners, do not understand the question of money.

I wish therefore to explain "money" in so simple a way that all can understand it.

Perhaps someone in the vast audience which I have imagined I am about to hold spellbound cries out: "Who are you, a gold-bug, a millionaire, an iron-baron, a beneficiary of the McKinley Bill?" Before beginning my address, let me therefore reply to that imaginary gentleman that I have not seen a thousand dollars in gold for many a year and that as an American manufacturer I intend to struggle still against the foreigner for the home market, even with the lower duties fixed upon our product by that bill, and that I am not in favor of protection beyond the point necessary to allow Americans to retain their own market in a fair contest with the foreigner.

It does not matter who the man is, nor what he does, be he worker in the mine, factory or field, farmer, laborer, merchant, manufacturer, millionaire; he is deeply interested in understanding **this question of money**, and in having the right policy adopted about it. Therefore, I ask all to hear what I have to say, because what is good for one worker must be good for all, and what injures one must injure all, poor or rich.

To get at the root of the subject, you must know, first, why money exists. Secondly, you must know what money really is.

Let me try to tell you how money comes. In times past, when the people only tilled the soil, and commerce and manufactures had not developed, men had few wants, and so they got along without "money" by exchanging the articles themselves when they needed something which they had not. The farmer who wanted a pair of shoes gave so many bushels of corn for them, and his wife bought her sunbonnet by giving so many bushels of potatoes. Thus, all sales and purchases were made by exchanging articles, by bartering.

As population grew and wants extended, this plan became very inconvenient. One man in the district then started a general store and kept on hand a great many of the things which were most wanted and took for these any of the articles which the farmer had to give in exchange. This was a great step in advance, for the farmer who wanted half a dozen different things when he went to the village had no longer to search for half a dozen different people who wanted one or more of the things he had to offer in exchange. He could now go directly to one man, the storekeeper, and for any of his agricultural products he could get most of the articles he desired.

It did not matter to the storekeeper whether he gave the farmer tea or coffee, blankets or a hay rake. Nor did it matter what articles he took from the farmer, wheat or corn or potatoes, so he could send them away to the city and get other articles for them which he wanted. The farmer could even pay the wages of his hired men by giving them orders for articles upon the store. No dollars appear here yet. All is still barter, exchange of articles, very inconvenient and very costly because the agricultural articles given in exchange had to be hauled about and were always changing their value.

One day the storekeeper would be willing to take, say, a bushel of wheat for so many pounds of sugar; but upon the next visit of the farmer, it might be impossible for him to do so. He might require more wheat for the same amount of sugar. But if the market for wheat had risen and not fallen, you may be sure the storekeeper didn't take less wheat as promptly as he required more. Just the same with any of the articles which the farmer had to offer. These went up and down in value; so did the tea and the coffee, and the sugar and the clothing, and the boots and the shoes which the storekeeper had for exchange.

It's needless to remark that in all these dealings the storekeeper had the advantage of the farmer. He knew the markets and their ups and downs long before the farmer did, and he knew the signs of the times better than the farmer or any of his customers could. The storekeeper had the inside track all the time. Just here I wish you to note particularly that the storekeeper liked to take one article from the farmer better than another; that article being always the one for which the storekeeper had the best customers, something that was most in demand. In Virginia that article came to be tobacco. Over a great portion of our country it was wheat, whence comes the saying, "As good as wheat." It was taken everywhere, because it could be most easily disposed of for anything else desired.

What we now call "money" was not much used then in the West or the South, but you see that in its absence experience had driven the people to select some one article to use for exchanging other articles, and that this was wheat in Pennsylvania and tobacco in Virginia. This was done, not through any legislation, but simply because experience had proved the necessity for making the one thing serve as "money" which had proved itself best as a basis in paying for a farm or for affecting any exchange of things. Further, different articles were found best for the purpose in different regions. The people had voted for wheat and made it their money, and because tobacco was the principal crop in Virginia, the people there found it the best for using as money in that State.

BUILDING TO LAST

Please observe that in all cases human society chooses for that which we call "money" that which fluctuates least in price; is the most generally used or desired; is in the most constant demand; and has value in itself.

Money is only a word meaning the article used as the basis article for exchanging all other articles. An article is not first made valuable by law and then elected to be money. The article first proves itself valuable and best suited for the purpose and so becomes of itself and in itself the basis article — money. It elects itself. Wheat and tobacco were just as clearly money when used as the basis-article as gold and silver are money now.

We take one step further. The country becomes more and more populous, the wants of the people more and more numerous. The use of bulky products like wheat and tobacco, changeable in value, liable to decay, and of different grades, is soon found troublesome and unsuited for the growing business of exchange of articles, and they are therefore unfit to be longer used as money. You see at once that we could not get along today with grain as money.

The A-B-C's of Money

Then metals proved their superiority. These do not decay, do not change in value so rapidly, and they share with wheat and tobacco the one essential quality of having value in themselves for other purposes than for the mere basis of exchange. People want them for personal adornment or in manufactures and the arts – for a thousand uses. It is this very fact that makes them suitable for use as money. Just try to count how many purposes gold is needed for, because it is best suited for those purposes. It meets us everywhere. We cannot even get married without the ring of gold.

Because metals have a value in the open market, being desired for other uses than for the one use as money, and because the supply of these is limited and cannot be increased as easily as that of wheat or tobacco, these metals are less liable to fluctuate in value than any article previously used as money. This is of vital importance, for the one essential quality that is needed in the article which we use as a basis for exchanging all other articles is fixity of value. The race has instinctively always sought for the one article in the world which most resembles the North Star among the other stars in the heavens and used it as money. The article that changes least in value, as the North Star is the star which changes its position least in the heavens; and what the North Star is among stars the article people elect as money is among articles. All other articles revolve around it, as all other stars revolve around the North Star.

We have proceeded so far that we have now dropped all perishable articles and **elected metals as our money** or, rather, metals have proved themselves better than anything else for the standard of value, money.

Another great step had to be taken. When I was in China, I received as change, shavings and chips cut from a bar of silver and weighed before my eyes in the scales of the merchant, for the Chinese have no coined money. In Siam "cowries" are used — pretty little shells which the natives use as ornaments. Twelve of these represent a cent in value. You can well see how impossible it was for me to prevent the Chinese dealer from giving me less than the amount of silver to which I was entitled, or the Siam dealer from giving me poor shells, of the value of which I knew nothing.

Civilized nations soon felt the necessity of having their governments take certain quantities of the metals and stamp upon them the evidence of their weight, purity, and real value. Thus came the minting of metals into money — a great advance. People then knew at sight the exact value of each piece, and could no longer be cheated, no weighing or testing being necessary. Note that the government stamp did not add any value to the coin. The government did not attempt to make money out of nothing. It only told the people the market value of the metal in each coin, just what the metal, the raw material, could be sold for as metal and not as money.

Here swindling still occurs. Rogues cut the edges and then beat the coins out, so that many of these became very light. A clever Frenchman invented the milling of the edges of the coins, whereby this robbery was stopped, and civilized nations had at last the coinage which still remains with us, the most perfect ever known, because it is of high value in itself and changes least.

An ideally perfect article for use as money is one that never changes. This is essential for the protection of the workers — the farmers, mechanics, and all who labor. For nothing tends to make every exchange of articles a speculation so much as money which changes in value, and in the game of speculation, the masses of people are always sure to be beaten by the few who deal in money and know most about it.

Nothing places the farmer, the wage-earner, and all those not closely connected with financial affairs at so great a disadvantage in disposing of their labor or products as changeable money. All such are exactly in the position occupied by the farmer trading with the storekeeper as before described. Fish will not rise to the fly in calm weather. It is when the wind blows, and the surface is ruffled, that the poor victim mistakes the lure for a genuine fly. So it is with the business affairs of the world.

In stormy times, when prices are going up and down, when the value of the article used as money is dancing about – up today, down tomorrow – and the waters are troubled. The clever speculator catches the fish and fills his basket with the victims. Hence the farmer and the mechanic, and all people having crops to sell or receiving salaries or wages, are those most deeply interested in securing and maintaining fixity of value in the article they must take as money.

The A-B-C's of Money

But I am now to tell you another quality which this basis-article of metal has proved itself to possess, which you will find very difficult to believe. The whole world has such confidence in its fixity of value that there has been built upon it, as upon a sure foundation, **a tower of credit** so high, so vast, that all the silver and gold in the United States, and all the greenbacks and notes issued by the government only perform 8% of the exchanges of the country.

Go into any bank, trust, mill, factory, store, or place of business, and you will find that for every $100,000 of business transacted, only about $8,000 dollars of money is used, and this only for petty purchases and payments. 92% of the business is done with little bits of paper, checks, and drafts. Upon this basis also rests all the government bonds, all State, county, and city bonds, and the thousands of millions of bonds the sale of which has enabled our great railway systems to be built and the thousands of millions of the earnings of the masses deposited in savings banks, which have been lent by these banks to various parties and which must be returned in good money, else the poor depositor's savings will be partially or wholly lost.

BUILDING TO LAST

The business and exchanges of the country are not done now with money itself. Just as in former days the articles themselves ceased to be exchanged, and a metal called money was used to affect the exchanges, so today the metal itself — "the money" — is no longer used. The check or draft of the buyer of articles upon a store of gold deposited in a bank — a little bit of paper — is all that passes between the buyer and the seller. Why is this bit of paper taken by the seller or the one to whom there is debt due?

Because the taker is confident that if he really needed the article itself that it calls for, the gold, he could get it. He is confident also that he will not need the article itself, and why? Because for what he wishes to buy the seller or any man whom he owes will take his cheque, a similar little bit of paper, instead of gold itself. Then, most vital of all, everyone is confident that the basis-article cannot change in value. For remember, it would be almost as bad if it rose in value as if it fell. Steadiness of value being one essential quality in money for the masses of the people.

When, therefore, people clamor for more money to be put in circulation, see that more money is not so much what is needed. Nobody who has had wheat or tobacco or any article to sell has ever found any trouble for want of money in the hands of the buyer to effect the exchange. We had a very severe financial disturbance in this country only three months ago. Money, it was said, could not be had for business purposes, but it was not the metal itself that was lacking, but credit, i.e. confidence. For upon that, as you have seen, all business is done except small purchases and payments which can scarcely be called business at all.

Today the businessman cannot walk the street with-out being approached by people begging him to take this credit at very low rates of interest: at 2% per annum, credit can be had day by day. There has been no considerable difference in the amount of money in existence during the ninety days. There was about as much money in the country in January as there is in March. It was not the want of money, then, that caused the trouble.

The foundation had been shaken upon which stood the $92,000 of every $100,000 of business. The metal itself and notes — real money, as we have seen — only apply to the $8,000. Here comes the gravest of all dangers in tampering with the basis. You shake directly the foundation upon which rests 92% of all the business exchanges of the country, confidence, credit, and indirectly the trifling 8% as well which is transacted by the exchange of the metal itself or by government notes; for the standard article is the foundation for every exchange, both the $92,000 and the $8,000.

So, you see, if that is undermined, the vast structure, comprising all business built upon it, must totter and fall.

Reflection Section

The ABC's of Money

In this chapter, Carnegie strips away confusion about money and explains its true purpose: a stable, widely accepted foundation for fair exchange. He walks readers through the evolution of money: from bartering with wheat and tobacco to the modern reliance on gold-backed credit, emphasizing that money should have **intrinsic value, stability**, and inspire **confidence**. Carnegie's real concern is not abstract economics but protecting working people, those most vulnerable when money is manipulated or misunderstood.

He cautions against seeing money as something the government can magically create and instead reminds readers that **confidence and credit**, rooted in trust, drive most transactions. At its core, this chapter is a call for **financial wisdom, personal** responsibility, and vigilance against monetary instability, especially for those who labor and save.

Guided Reflection

1. "What is money, really?"

Carnegie argues that money is not created by law but chosen by people because of its stability and real-world usefulness.

- What does this understanding of money change about how you view your own finances, investments, or savings?

- Are you currently building your financial life on something stable and trusted?

2. "Confidence is the foundation."

Over 90% of economic activity, he says, is based not on actual money, but on **trusting in** institutions, credit, and consistency.

- Where in your financial or professional life do you rely most on trust or credit?

- How are you cultivating trustworthiness in the way you do business or manage money?

3. "Money that changes value is a trap." Volatile currency both benefits speculators and harms workers. Carnegie stands firmly for stability.

- In your own experience, when have you felt the effects of economic uncertainty?

- How can you prepare for instability while still building long-term financial health?

4. "Workers understand the system." Carnegie believed that the misunderstanding of money is one of the greatest threats to the average person's success.

- What financial principles do you wish you had learned earlier in life?

- What could you pass onto your family, your team, or your community—to help others become financially literate?

Chapter 3

On Common Interest of Labor & Capital

A great philosopher has pointed out to us that in this life the chief and highest reward that we can obtain is the purchase of satisfactions. I have purchased a great satisfaction, one of the greatest I have ever acquired: I have been privileged to help some of my fellow-workmen help themselves. This library [1] will give them an opportunity to make themselves more valuable to their employers and so lay up intellectual capital that cannot be impaired or depreciated.

It is very unfortunate that the irresistible tendency of our age, which draws manufacturing into immense establishments, requiring the work of thousands of men, renders it impossible for employers

---

[1] This essay stems from an address to workmen at the dedication of the Carnegie Library, Braddock, Pa., January 1889.

who reside near to obtain that intimate acquaintance with employees which, under the old system of manufacturing in very small establishments, made the relation of master and man more pleasing to both.

When articles were manufactured in small shops by employers who required only the assistance of a few men and apprentices, the employer had opportunities to know everyone, to become well acquainted with each, to know his merits both as a man and as a workman. On the other hand, the workman being brought into closer contact with his employer, inevitably knew more of his business, his cares and troubles, and more important than all, they came to know something of the characteristics of the man himself.

All this has changed.

Today employees become more and more like human machines to the employer, and the employer becomes almost a myth to his men. From every point of view this is a most regrettable result, yet it is one for which I see no remedy. The free play of economic laws is forcing the manufacture of all articles of general consumption more and more into the hands of a few enormous monopolies, that their cost to the consumer may be less.

It being therefore impossible for the employers of thousands to become acquainted with their men, if we are not to lose all feeling of mutuality between us, **the employer must seek their acquaintance through other forms**, to express his care for the well-being of those upon whose labor he depends for success by devoting part of his earnings for institutions like this library, and I hope in return that the employees are to show by the use which they make of such benefactions that they in turn respond to this sentiment upon the part of employers wherever it may be found.

By such means as these we may hope to maintain to some extent the old feeling of kindliness, mutual confidence, respect and esteem which formerly distinguished the relations between the employer and his men. We are younger than Europe and have still something to see from the older land in this respect, but I rejoice to see that many manufacturers in this country are awaking to the sense of duty to their employees. What is even still more important are the evidence which we find among our workmen of a desire to establish societies which cannot but be beneficial to themselves. It is all well enough for people to help others, but the grandest result is achieved when people prove able to help themselves.

Believe me, **the interests of capital and labor are one.** He is an enemy of labor who seeks to array labor against capital. He is an enemy of capital who seeks to array capital against labor. The greatest cause of the friction which prevails between capital and labor, the real essence of the trouble, and the remedy I propose for this unfortunate friction is as follows:

Wages should be based on a sliding scale of success or failure of the company.

Allow me to explain.

The trouble is that men are not paid at any time the compensation proper to that time. All large companies necessarily keep filled with orders in advance, and these orders are taken at prices prevailing when they are booked. For example, steel rails at the end of last year for delivery this year were $29 per ton at the works. Of course, the mills entered orders freely at this price and kept on entering them until the demand growing unexpectedly great carried prices up to $35 per ton. The various mills in America are compelled for the next six months or more to run upon orders which do not average $31 per ton. Transportation, ironstone, and prices of all kinds have advanced upon them in the meantime, and they must therefore run for the bulk of the year upon very small margins of profit. But the men noticing in the papers "the great boom in steel rails," very naturally demand their share of the advance, and under our existing faulty arrangements between capital and labor they have secured it.

The employers, therefore, have grudgingly given what they know under proper arrangements they should not have been required to give. And there has been friction and still is dissatisfaction upon the part of the employers.

Reverse this picture: The steel-rail market falls again. The mills have still six months' work at prices above the prevailing market and can afford to pay men higher wages than the then existing state of the market would apparently justify. But having just been immersed in extra payments for labor which they should not have paid, they naturally attempt to reduce wages as the market price of rails goes down, and thence arises discontent among the men, and we have a repetition of the negotiations and strikes which have characterized the beginning of this year.

In other words, **when the employer is going down the employee insists on going up, and vice versa**. What we must seek is a plan by which men will receive high wages when their employers are receiving high prices for the product and hence are making large profits and, per contra, when the employers are receiving low prices for product and therefore small if any profits, the men will receive low wages.

If this plan can be found, employers and employees will be in the same boat, rejoicing together in their prosperity and calling into play their fortitude together in a diversity. There will be no room for quarrels, and instead of a feeling of antagonism, there will be a feeling of partnership between employers and the employed. There is a simple means of producing this result, and to its general introduction both employers and employees should steadily bend their energies: Wages should be based upon a sliding scale, in proportion to the net prices received for product month by month. It is impossible for capital to defraud labor under a sliding scale.

Common Interest

One advantage of this library will be that it will bring before you every local newspaper and every trade journal, and I beg you all to read these carefully. You will find many misstatements and blunders. These are inseparable from the newspaper press, which must work hastily and report even rumors. But by studying the principal journals the tendency of affairs can be correctly seen. Newspapers will not give you a correct statement of the prices of material. Manufacturers are disposed to give the brightest coloring to the situation, to report the highest sales made with a view to maintain prices and induce customers to purchase. They will probably not report how low they have been compelled to sell in order to meet competition and keep works running.

Nevertheless, careful perusal of the newspapers and trade journals will enable you to form a general opinion of the trend of events in the commercial world. If you read the papers today, you will know that out of thirteen mills engaged in the manufacture of steel rails in this country, not more than three are running to their capacity. Only one mill in all the West is making rails, and I am sorry to say that it seems probable that even that one will not be able to run continuously.

BUILDING TO LAST

The melancholiest feature in all the disputes between labor and capital is that it is scarcely ever capital that succeeds in breaking down the price of labor: it is labor which stabs labor. Look around you and see labor working for 20% and even 30% less in some mills, and at Johnstown and Harrisburg for less than one-half what we pay for skilled labor in this district. Then in your hearts blame not capital, but consider employers who regret those reductions in wages, who stand out against them and run for years at higher prices, as the best friends of labor, even although at last they must frankly confess that if they are to give their men steady employment and save their capital and works, they are forced to ask them to work at the rates obtained by their competitors. The first employer who reduces labor is labor's enemy, but the last employer to reduce labor may be labor's staunchest friend.

The fatal enemy of labor is labor, not capital.

The greatest character in the public life of Britain, and the staunchest friend of that republic in its hour of need, the radical, John Bright, being once asked what his most valuable acquisition was, replied, "A taste for reading." I can truthfully say from my own experience that I agree with that great man.

Most anxious to give you the best advice in my power, I advise you to **cultivate the taste for reading**. When I was a boy in my teens in Allegheny City, Col. Anderson, whose memory I must ever revere, who had a few hundred books, gave notice that he would lend these books every Saturday afternoon to boys and young men. You cannot imagine with what anxiety some of us embraced this opportunity to obtain knowledge. I looked forward to every Saturday afternoon, when we could get one book exchanged for another. The principal partner with me in all our business, Mr. Phipps, equally with myself, had obtained access to the stores of knowledge by means of this benefactor.

It is from personal experience that I feel that there is no human arrangement so powerful for good, there is no benefit that can be bestowed upon a community so great, as that which places within the reach of all the treasures of the world which are stored up in books.

BUILDING TO LAST

We occasionally find traces even today of the old prejudice which existed against educating the masses of the people. I do not wonder that this should exist when I reflect upon what has hitherto passed for education. Men have wasted their precious years trying to extract education from an ignorant past whose chief province is to teach us, not what to adopt, but what to avoid. Men have sent their sons to colleges to waste their energies upon obtaining a knowledge of such languages as Greek and Latin, which are of no more practical use to them than Choctaw. I have met few college graduates that knew Shakespeare or Milton. They might be able to tell you all about Ulysses or Agamemnon or Hector, but what are these compared to the characters that we find in our own classics?

One service Russell Lowell has done, for which he should be thanked, has boldly said that in Shakespeare alone we have a greater treasure than in all the classics of ancient times. They have been crammed with the details of petty and insignificant skirmishes between savages and taught to exalt a band of ruffians into heroes, and we have called them "educated".

They have been "educated" as if they were destined for life upon some other planet than this. They have in no sense received instruction. On the contrary, what they have obtained has served to imbue them with false ideas and to give them a distaste for practical life. I do not wonder that a prejudice has arisen and still exists against such education. In my own experience I can say that I have known few young men intended for business who were not injured by a collegiate education. Had they gone into active work during the years spent at college they would have been better educated men in every true sense of that term.

The fire and energy have been stamped out of them, and how to so manage as to live a life of idleness and not a life of usefulness has become the chief question with them. But a new idea of education is now upon us.

We have begun to realize that a knowledge of chemistry, for instance, is worth a knowledge of all the dead languages that ever were spoken upon the earth; a knowledge of mechanics more useful than all the classical learning that can be crammed into young men at college. What is the young man to do who knows Greek with the young man that knows stenography or telegraphy, bookkeeping or chemistry, or the law of mechanics? Not that any kind of knowledge is to be underrated. All knowledge is, in a sense, useful. The point I wish to make is this, that, except for the few who have the taste of the antiquarian, and who find that their work in life is to delve among the dusty records of the past, and for the few that lead professional lives, the education given today in our colleges is a positive disadvantage.

The lack of education in its true sense has done more than all the other causes combined to prevent the universal recognition of labor. I remember that the great president, the greatest of all railway managers, Edgar Thomson, after whom the works here are called, once asked me to remove from Pittsburg to be master of machinery of the Pennsylvania Railroad.

Well, you may smile. And I said to Mr. Thomson, "Why, Mr. Thomson, you amaze me. I know nothing whatever about machinery."

"That is the reason I want you to take charge of it, he replied. I have never known a mechanic with judgment and good sense except one."

This lack of judgment in mechanics was because at that day in this country they had failed to receive an all-round education. I mean the true education and knowledge of matters and things in general, by which we are surrounded and with which we must deal. If you want to make labor what it should be, educate yourself in useful knowledge. That is the moral I would emphasize. Get knowledge. Cultivate a taste for reading, that you may know what the world has done and is doing and the drift of affairs.

The value of the education which young men can now receive cannot be overestimated, and it is to this education, as given in technical schools, to which I wish to call your attention. Time was when men had so little knowledge that it was easy for one man to embrace it all, and the courses in colleges bear painful evidence of this fact today. Knowledge is now so various, so extensive, so minute, that it is impossible for any man to know thoroughly more than one small branch. **This is the age of the specialist**. Therefore, you who must make your living in this world should resolve to know the art which gives you support; to know that thoroughly and well to be an expert in your specialty.

If you are a mechanic, then from this library study every work bearing upon the subject of mechanics. If you are a chemist, then every work bearing upon chemistry. If in the mines, then every work upon mining. Let no man know more of your specialty than you do yourself. That should be your ideal. Then, far less important, but still important, to bring sweetness and light into your life, be sure to read widely, and know a little about as many things as you have time to read about. Just as on his farm the farmer must first attend well to his potatoes and his corn and his wheat, from which he derives his revenue, and he may spend his spare hours as a labor of love in cultivating the flowers that surround his home, so too for you: one domain your work, and the other your recreation.

In these days of transition and struggle between labor and capital, to no better purpose can you devote a few of your spare hours than to **the study of economic questions**. There are certain great laws which will be obeyed: the law of supply and demand; the law of competition; the law of wages and of profits. All these you will find laid down in the textbooks. Remember that there is no more possibility of defeating the operation of these laws than there is of thwarting the laws of nature which determine the humidity of the atmosphere or the revolution of the earth upon its axis.

Common Interest

The severe study of scientific books must not be permitted to exclude the equally important duty of reading the masters in literature. The feeling which prevails in some quarters against fiction is, in my opinion, only a prejudice. I know that some, indeed most, of the most eminent men find in a good work of fiction one of the best means of enjoyment and of rest. When exhausted in mind and body, and especially in mind, nothing is so beneficial to them as to read a good novel. It is no disparagement of free libraries that most of the works read are works of fiction. On the contrary, it is doubtful if any other form of literature would so well serve the important end of lifting hard-working men out of the prosaic and routine duties of life.

The works of Scott, Thackeray, Eliot, Dickens, Hawthorne, and others of the same class, are not to be rated below any other form of literature for workingmen.

You all know how much manufacturing science is indebted to the improvements and inventions which owe their first suggestion to the workman himself. Now mark this important fact. These improvements and inventions come from the educated — educated in the true sense — and never from the ignorant workman.

BUILDING TO LAST

They must come, and they do come, from men who are in their special department men of more knowledge than their fellows. If they have not read, then they have observed, which is the best form of education.

The important fact is that they must know that *how* the knowledge was acquired matters not. The fact that they know more about a problem than their fellows and can suggest the remedy or improvement is what is of value to them and their employer. There is no means so sure for enabling the workman to rise to the foremanship, managership, and finally partnership as knowledge of all that has been done and is being done in the world today in the special department in which he labors.

From the highest down to the lowest a better grade of service is rendered by the intelligent man than it is possible for the ignorant man to render. His knowledge always comes in, and whether you have knowledge, on the part of the manager who directs, or of the man who only handles a shovel, you have in him a valuable employee in proportion to his knowledge, other things being equal. During my experience as a manufacturer, I know our firm has made many mistakes by neglecting one simple rule, "never to undertake anything new until your managers have had an opportunity to examine everything that has been done throughout this world in that department."

Neglect of this has cost us many hundreds of thousands of dollars, and we have become wise. Now I say here to the man who is ambitious to learn, who, perhaps, thinks that he has some improvement in his mind, here in the rooms of this library, there is, or I hope soon will be, the whole world's experience upon that subject brought right before you down to a recent date. In any question of mechanics or any question of chemistry you will find the records of the world at your disposal here. If you are on the wrong track, these books will tell you; if you are on the right track, they will tell you. You can go through hall after hall in the patent office in Washington and see thousands of models of inventions bearing upon all branches of human industry, and ninety-nine out of every hundred would never have been placed there had the ignorant inventor had at command such facilities as will be yours in this library.

I have heard employers say that there was great danger that the masses of the people might become too well educated to be content in their useful and necessary occupations. It has required an effort upon my part to listen to this doctrine with patience. It is all wrong; I give it an unqualified contradiction.

The trouble between capital and labor is just in proportion to the ignorance of the employer and the ignorance of the employed. The more intelligent the employer the better, and the more intelligent the employed the better. It is never education, it is never knowledge, that produces collision. It is always ignorance on the part of one or the other of the two forces. Speaking from an experience not inconsiderable, I make this statement:

Capital is ignorant of the necessities and the just dues of labor, and labor is ignorant of the necessities and dangers of capital.

That is the true origin of friction between them. More knowledge on the part of capital of the good qualities of those that serve it, and some knowledge upon the part of the men of the economic laws which hold the capitalists in their relentless grasp, would obviate most of the difficulties which arise between these two forces, which are indispensably necessary to each other. I hope that those of our men who possess that inestimable prize, the taste for reading, will make it a point to study carefully a few of the fundamental laws from which there is no escape, either on the part of capital or labor.

If this library be instrumental in the slightest degree in spreading knowledge in this department, it will have justified its existence. I trust that you will not forget the importance of amusements. **Life must not be taken too seriously**. It is a great mistake to think that the man who works all the time wins in the race. Have your amusements. Learn to play a good game of whist or a good game of drafts, or a good game of billiards.

Become interested in baseball or cricket, or horses, anything that will give you innocent enjoyment and relieve you from the usual strain. There is not anything better than a good laugh. I attribute most of my success in life to the fact that, as my partners often say, trouble runs off my back like water from a duck. There is a poetical quotation from Shakespeare, that is applicable. It is to "wear your troubles like your garments, carelessly."

BUILDING TO LAST

Many men are to be met with in this life who would have been great and successful had the world rated them at the value which they placed upon themselves. This class are the victims of an hallucination. Nobody in the world desires to keep down ability. Everybody in the world has an outstretched hand for it. Every employer of labor is studying the young men around him, most anxious to find one of exceptional ability. Nothing in the world so desirable for him and so profitable for him as such a man. Every manager in the works stands ready to grasp, to utilize the man that can do something that is valuable.

Every foreman wants to have under him in his department able men upon whom he can rely and whose merits he obtains credit for, because the greatest test of ability in a manager is not the man himself, but the men with whom he is able to surround himself.

These books on the shelves will tell you the story of the rise of many men from our own ranks. It is not the educated, or so-called, classically educated man, it is not the aristocracy, it is not the monarchs, that have ruled the destinies of the world, either in camp, laboratory or workshop. The great inventions, the improvements, the discoveries in science, the great works in literature have sprung from the ranks of the poor. You can scarcely name a great invention, or a great discovery, you can scarcely name a great picture, or a great statue, a great song or a great story, nor anything great that has not been the product of men who started to earn an honest living by honest work.

Believe me, the man whom the foreman does not appreciate, and the foreman whom the manager does not appreciate, and the manager whom the firm does not appreciate, has to find the fault not in the firm, or the manager, or the foreman, but in himself. He cannot give the service that which is so invaluable and so anxiously looked for. There is no man who may not rise to the highest position, nor is there any man who, from lack of the right qualities or failure to exercise them, may not sink to the lowest.

Employees have chances to rise to higher work, to rise to foreman, to be superintendents, and even to rise to be partners, and even to be chairmen in our service, if they prove themselves possessed of the qualities required. They need never fear being dispensed with. It is we who fear that the abilities of such men may be lost to us.

BUILDING TO LAST

It is highly gratifying to know that the hours of labor are being gradually reduced throughout the country — eight hours to work, eight hours to play, eight hours to sleep, seems the ideal division. You need not work twelve hours very long. Most of us worked more hours than twelve in our youth. The workman has many advantages today over his predecessors. A sliding scale for his labor ranks him higher than before as a man and a citizen. The proportion of the joint earnings of capital and labor given to labor was never so great and is constantly rising, the earnings of capital were never so low. The cost of living never was so low in recent times.

I hope the future will add many more advantages and that the toilsome march which labor has had to make on its way from serfdom, when our forefathers were bought and sold with the mines and factories they worked, up to its present condition, is not yet ended, but that it is destined to continue and lead to other important results for the benefit and dignity of labor.

Reflection Section

On Common Interest of Labor & Capital

In this impassioned address, Carnegie argues for a shift in how workers and employers relate—not through conflict, but through shared understanding, responsibility, and long-term investment in each other. He proposes a sliding wage scale to align the fortunes of labor and capital, removing antagonism by creating common cause. He calls for education, self-improvement, and cultural enrichment as the foundations for both dignity and advancement in the labor force.

Carnegie critiques hollow classical education, emphasizing instead practical, applied knowledge and self-driven learning. He reminds workers that the greatest advancements, inventions, discoveries, or works of art, have often come from those who began with little more than determination and a willingness to grow. The path to partnership, leadership, and legacy lies not in agitation, but in mastery and character.

BUILDING TO LAST

Guided Reflection

1. **"We are in the same boat."** Carnegie insists that both depend on each other and suffer when pitted against one another.

- In your own work or leadership experience, how have you seen misunderstandings create unnecessary conflict?

- What can you do to foster a sense of shared mission between the people you work with or lead?

2. **"The sliding scale of wages."** He offers a bold solution: wages that rise and fall with the success of the business.

- How might your own business, team, or industry benefit from more transparent and flexible compensation models?

- What risks or benefits do you see in tying earnings to long-term outcomes?

3. "Education in the true sense."

Carnegie values knowledge that equips people to succeed in their chosen field, not abstract learning for its own sake.

- What kind of learning are you actively pursuing right now?

- How might you deepen your expertise or broaden your thinking to become more valuable in your work or calling?

4. "Ignorance is the root of friction."

He asserts that most conflict between capital and labor comes from ignorance on both sides.

- Have you ever misjudged someone else's position because of limited understanding?

- What steps can you take to become better informed about the challenges faced by those above or below you in the structure of your work?

5. "Ignorance is the root of friction." II

Carnegie affirms the potential in every worker, emphasizing merit, discipline, and visibility.

- In your own journey, what steps have helped you grow or gain recognition?

- Who around you might be ready to rise, if given encouragement or opportunity?

Chapter 4

Thrift as Duty

The habit of thrift constitutes one of the greatest differences between the savage and the civilized man. One of the fundamental differences between savage and civilized life is the absence of thrift in the one and the presence of it in the other.

When millions of men each save a little of their daily earnings, these petty sums combined make an enormous amount, which is called capital, about which so much is written. If men consumed each day of each week all they earned, as does the savage, of course there would be no capital – no savings laid up for future use. Now, let us see what capital does in the world.

We will consider what the shipbuilders do when they have to build great ships. These enterprising companies offer to build an ocean greyhound for, let us say, £500,000, to be paid only when the ship is delivered after satisfactory trial trips. Where or how do the shipbuilders get this sum of money to pay the workmen, the wood merchant, the steel manufacturer, and all the people who furnish material for the building of the ship? They get it from the savings of civilized men. It is part of the money saved for investment by the millions of industrious people. Each man, by thrift, saves a little, puts the money in a bank, and the bank lends it to the shipbuilders, who pay interest for the use of it.

It is the same with the building of a factory, a railroad, a canal, or anything costly. We could not have had anything more than the savage had, except for thrift. Hence, thrift is mainly at the bottom of an improvement. Without it no railroads, no canals, no ships, no telegraphs, no churches, no universities, no schools, no newspapers, nothing great or costly could we have. Man must exercise thrift and save before he can produce anything material of great value. There was nothing built, no great progress made, as long as man remained a thriftless savage. The civilized man has no clearer duty than from early life to keep steadily in view the necessity of providing for the future of himself and those dependent upon him.

There are few rules more salutary than that which has been followed by most wise and good men, namely, "that **expenses should always be less than income**." In other words, one should be a civilized man, saving something, and not a savage, consuming every day all that which he has earned. The great poet, Bums, in his advice to a young man, says:

> To catch Dame Fortune's golden smile,
> Assiduous wait upon her:
> And gather gear by every wile
> That's justified by honor.
> Not for to hide it in a hedge.
> Not for a train attendant;
> But for the glorious privilege
> Of being independent.

That is sound advice, so far as it goes, and I hope the reader will take it to heart and adopt it. No proud, self-respecting person can ever be happy, or even satisfied, who has to be dependent upon others for his necessary wants. He who is dependent has not reached the full measure of manhood and can hardly be counted among the worthy citizens of the republic. The safety and progress of our country depend not upon the highly educated men, nor the few millionaires, nor upon the greater number of the extreme poor; but upon the mass of sober, intelligent, industrious and saving workers, who are neither very rich nor very poor.

Thrift Duty Has Its Limit

As a rule, you will find that the saving man is a temperate man, a good husband and father, a peaceful, law-abiding citizen. Nor need the saving be great. It is surprising how little it takes to provide for the real necessities of life. A little home paid for and a few hundred dollars make all the difference. These are more easily acquired by frugal people than you might suppose. Great wealth is quite another and a far less desirable matter. It is not the aim of thrift, nor the duty of men to acquire millions. It is in no respect a virtue to set this before us as an end. Our duty is to save ends when just enough money has been put aside to provide comfortably for those dependent upon us. Hoarding millions is avarice, not thrift.

Of course, under our industrial conditions, it is inevitable that a few, a very few men, will find money coming to them far beyond their wants. The accumulation of millions is usually the result of enterprise and judgment, and some exceptional ability for organization. It does not come from savings in the ordinary sense of that word. Men who in old age strive only to increase their already great hoards, are usually slaves of the habit of hoarding formed in their youth. At first they own the money they have made and saved. Later in life the money owns them, and they cannot help themselves, so overpowering is the force of habit, either for good or evil. It is the abuse of the civilized saving instinct and not its use, that produces this class of men.

No one need be afraid of falling victim to this abuse of the habit if he always; bears in mind that whatever surplus wealth may come to him is to be regarded as a sacred trust, which he is bound to administer for the good of his fellows The man should always be master. He should keep money in the position of a useful servant. He must never let it master and make a miser of him.

A man's first duty is to have competence and be independent. But his whole duty does not end here. It is his duty to do something for his needy neighbors who are less favored than himself. It is his duty to contribute to the general good of the community in which he lives. He has been protected by its laws. Because he has been protected in his various enterprises, he has been able to make money sufficient for his needs and those of his family. All beyond this belongs in justice to the protecting power that has fostered him and enabled him to win wealth.

To try to make the world in some way better than you found it, is to have a noble motive in life. Your surplus wealth should contribute to the development of your own character and place you in the ranks of nature's noblemen. It is no less than a duty for you to understand how important it is, and how clear your duty is, to form the habit of thrift. When you begin to earn, always save some part of your earnings, like a civilized man, instead of spending all, like the poor savage.

Reflection Section

Thrift as Duty

In this brief but potent chapter, Carnegie reframes thrift not as a financial tactic, but as a civic and moral obligation. Thrift, he argues, is the defining difference between a civilized and a savage society. By saving even modest amounts, individuals contribute to the capital that builds railroads, factories, and entire communities. The habit of saving enables not only personal independence, but also national progress.

Carnegie is careful to draw a line between wise saving and obsessive hoarding. Thrift is virtuous when it provides for one's family and enables generosity. It becomes a vice when wealth comes to an end in itself. His call is clear: save to serve. Cultivate the habit early, use money as a servant, and when your needs are met, give back.

BUILDING TO LAST

Guided Reflection

1. "Thrift is civilization."

Carnegie sees thrift as the foundation for all progress—personal, industrial, and national.

- How do your saving habits reflect your long-term goals, values, or responsibilities?

- Are you currently saving with purpose, or simply reacting to your financial circumstances?

2. "The man should be master."

Money, he warns, can shift from being a tool to being a tyrant.

- In what areas of your life does money serve you well?

- Are there any signs that it might be beginning to control you instead?

3. "Enough is enough."

Thrift's goal is not vast wealth, but independence and usefulness.

- Do you have a sense of what "enough" looks like for you and your family?

- What would change in your life if you focused less on accumulation and more on contribution?

4. "Your surplus is a trust."

Any wealth beyond your needs, Carnegie says, must be used for the good of others.

- What cause, community, or individual could benefit from your surplus— whether money, time, or knowledge?

- How might practicing generosity actually strengthen your own character?

BUILDING TO LAST

5. "Live like a civilized man."

To spend all that you earn is to fall short of your potential and your responsibility.

- What small habit or decision could you change this week to begin practicing greater thrift?

Chapter 5

How to Win Fortune

Labor is divided into two great armies: the agricultural and the industrial. In these, diverse forces are in operation. In the former, everything tends to the further distribution of land among the many; in the latter, everything tends to a concentration of business in the hands of the few. One of the two great fallacies upon which "Progress and Poverty" — Mr. George's book — is founded, is that the land is getting more and more into the hands of the few. Now the only source from which Mr. George could obtain correct information upon this point is the census; and this tells us that in 1850 the average extent of farms in the United States was 203 acres; in 1860, 199 acres; in 1870, 153 acres, and that in 1880 it was still further reduced to 134 acres. The reason is obvious for this rapid distribution of the land. The farmer who cultivates a small farm by his own labor is able to drive out of the field the ambitious capitalist who attempts to farm upon a large scale with the labor of others.

In Great Britain nothing has been more significant than that the tillers of small farms have passed through the agricultural depression there far better than those who cultivated large farms. So in both countries we have proof that under the free play of equal laws land is becoming more and more divided among the masses of the people. In the whole range of social questions no fact is more important than this, and nothing gives the thoughtful student greater satisfaction. The triumph of the small proprietor over the large proprietor insures the growth and maintenance of that element in society upon which civilization can most securely depend, for there is no force in a nation so conservative of what is good, so fair, so virtuous, as a race of men who till the soil they own. Happily for mankind experience proves that man cannot work more soil profitably than he can till himself with the aid of his own family.

When we turn to the other army of labor — the industrial — we are obliged to confess that it is swayed by the opposite law, which tends to concentrate manufacturing and business affairs generally in a few vast establishments. The fall in prices of manufactured articles has been startling. Never were the principal articles of consumption so low as they are today. This cheapening process is made possible only by concentration. We find 1,700 watches per day turned out by one company, and watches are sold for a few dollars apiece. We have mills making many thousand yards of calico per day, and this necessary article is to be had for a few cents per yard. Manufacturers of steel make 2,500 tons per day, and four pounds of finished steel are sold for 5 cents. And so on through the entire range of industries.

Divide the huge factories into smaller establishments, and it will be found impossible to manufacture some of the articles at all, the success of the process being often dependent on its being operated upon a large scale, while the cost of such articles as could be produced in small establishments would be two or three times their present prices. There does not appear to be any counteracting force to this law of concentration in the industrial world. On the contrary, the active forces at work seem to demand greater and greater output or turnover from each establishment in order that the minimum cost should be reached. Hence comes the rapid and continuous increase of the capital of manufacturing and commercial concerns, five, ten, fifteen, and even twenty million being sometimes massed in one corporation.

This has given rise to a complaint which is often heard, but which I hope to show has no foundation. The young practical man points to these and says to himself: "It is no longer possible for our class without capital to rise beyond the position of employees upon salaries. There is a lion in the path which leads to independent commands or to partnership, and this lion is the huge establishments already existing, which are an impassable barrier to our advancement."

The man engaged in the agricultural army, as we have seen, has nothing to fear from capital. With a small sum, which is not very difficult for him to save or borrow, he can begin farming, the only competition with which he has to contend being that of others of his own class situated like himself. It is certainly more difficult for a mechanic or practical man to establish a new business, or to win partnership in one that exists, than it is for the young farmer to begin his business; yet the difficulties are not insuperable, nor greater than have hitherto existed. They are not such as to stimulate the ambitious; and this is always to be taken into account, that if the race in the industrial and business world be harder to win, the prize is infinitely greater.

Before considering the prospects of the mechanic in the industrial, of the clerk in the mercantile, commercial and financial worlds, let me show that no classes other than these two have had much to do with establishing the factories, business houses and financial institutions which are best known in the United States today. And first, as to the part of trained mechanics. I select the best-known industrial establishments in each department, many of them the most extensive works of their kind and of worldwide reputation.

Every one of these great works was founded and managed by mechanics, men who served their apprenticeship. The list could be greatly extended, and if we were to include those which were created by men who entered life as office-boys or clerks, we should embrace almost every famous manufacturing concern in the country. Thomas Edison, for instance, was a telegraph operator. Corliss, of Corliss engine. Roebling, of wire fame, Spreckels, in sugar refining — all and many more captains of industry — were poor boys with natural aptitude, to whom a regular apprenticeship was scarcely necessary.

In banking and finance, it is an oft repeated story that our Stanfords, Rockefellers, Goulds, Sages, Fields, Dillons, Seligmans, Wilsons, and Huntingtons came from the ranks. The millionaires who are in active control started as poor boys and were trained in that sternest but most efficient of all schools — poverty.

College Graduates

I asked a city banker to give me a few names of presidents and vice-presidents and cashiers of our great New York city banks who had begun as boys or clerks. He sent me thirty-six names, and wrote he would send me more next day. The absence of the college graduate in the list should be deeply weighed. I have inquired and searched everywhere in all quarters but find small trace of him as the leader in affairs, although not seldom occupying positions of trust in financial institutions. Nor is this surprising.

How to Win Fortune

The prize-takers have too many years the start of the graduate; they have entered for the race invariably in their teens — in the most valuable of all the years for learning — from fourteen to twenty; while the college student has been learning a little about the barbarous and petty squabbles of a far-distant past, or trying to master languages which are dead, such knowledge as seems adapted for life upon another planet than this, as far as business affairs are concerned — the future captain of industry is hotly engaged in the school of experience, obtaining the very knowledge required for his future triumphs.

I do not speak of the effect of college education upon young men training for the learned professions, for which it is, up to a certain point, almost indispensable in our day for the average youth, but the almost total absence of the graduate from high position in the business world seems to justify the conclusion that college education as it exists seems almost fatal to success in that domain. It is to be noted that salaried officials are not in a strict sense in business — a captain of industry is one who makes his all in his business and depends upon success for compensation. It is in this field that the graduate has little chance, entering at twenty, against the boy who swept the office, or who begins as shipping clerk at fourteen. The facts prove this.

There are some instances of the sons of business men, graduates of colleges, who address themselves to a business life and succeed in managing a business already created, but even these are few compared with those who fail in keeping the fortune received. There has come, however, in recent years, the polytechnic and scientific school, or course of study, for boys, which is beginning to show most valuable fruits in the manufacturing branch. The trained mechanic of the past, who has, as we have seen, hitherto carried off most of the honors in our industrial works, is now to meet a rival in the scientifically educated youth, who will push him hard — very hard indeed. Three of the largest steel manufacturing concerns in the world are already under the management of three young, educated men — students of these schools who left theory at school for practice in the works while yet in their teens.

Most of the chiefs of departments under them are of the same class. Such young, educated men have one important advantage over the apprenticed mechanic — they are open-minded and without prejudice. The scientific attitude of mind, that of the searcher after truth, renders them receptive to new ideas. Great and invaluable as the working mechanic has been, and is, and will always be, yet he is disposed to adopt narrow views of affairs, for he is generally well up in years before he comes into power. It is different with the scientifically trained boy. He has no prejudices and goes in for the latest invention or newest method, no matter if another has discovered it. He adopts the plan that will beat the record and discards his own devices or ideas, which the working mechanic superintendent can rarely be induced to do. Let no one, therefore, underrate the advantage of education. Only it must be education adapted to the end in view and must give instruction bearing upon a man's career if he is to make his way to fortune.

Thus, in the financial, commercial and mercantile branches of business, as in manufacturing, we have to ask, not what place the educated mechanic and practical men occupy, but what these two types have left for others throughout the entire business world. Very little, indeed, have they left. In the industrial department the trained mechanic is the founder and manager of famous concerns. In the mercantile, commercial and financial it is the poor office-boy who has proved to be the merchant prince in disguise, who surely comes into his heritage. They are the winning classes.

It is the poor clerk and the working mechanic who finally rule in every branch of affairs, without capital, without family influence, and without college education. It is they who have risen to the top and taken command, who have abandoned salaried positions and boldly risked all in the founding of a business. College graduates will usually be found under salaries, trusted subordinates. Neither capital, nor influence, nor college learning, nor all combined have proved able to contend in business successfully against the energy and indomitable will which spring from all-conquering poverty. Lest anything here said may be construed as tending to decry or disparage university education let me clearly state that those addressed are the fortunate poor young men who have to earn a living. For such as can afford to obtain a university degree and have means sufficient to insure a livelihood, the writer is the last man to advise its rejection — compared with which all the pecuniary gains of the multi-millionaire are dross — but for poor youth the earning of a competence is a duty and duty done is worth even more than university education, precious as that is.

Liberal education gives a man who really absorbs it higher tastes and aims than the acquisition of wealth, and a world to enjoy, into which the mere millionaire cannot enter; to find therefore that it is not the best training for business is to prove its claim to a higher domain. True education can be obtained outside of the schools. Genius is not an indigenous plant in the groves academic, a wildflower found in the woods all by itself, needing no care from society – but average man needs universities.

Corporations

The young practical man of to-day working at the bench or counter, to whom the fair goddess, Fortune, has not yet beckoned, may be disposed to conclude that it is impossible to start business in this age. There is something in that. It is, no doubt, infinitely more difficult to start a new business of any kind today than it was. But it is only a difference in form, not in substance. It is infinitely easier for a young practical man of ability to obtain an interest in existing firms than it has ever been. The doors have not closed upon ability. On the contrary, they swing easier upon their hinges.

Capital is not requisite. Family influence, as before, passes for nothing. Real ability, the capacity for doing things, never was so eagerly searched for as now, and never commanded such rewards. The law which concentrates the leading industries and commercial, mercantile, and financial affairs in a few great factories or firms contains within itself another law not less imperious. These vast concerns cannot be successfully conducted by salaried employees. No great business of any kind can score an unusually brilliant and permanent success which is not in the hands of practical men pecuniarily interested in its results.

In the industrial world, the days of corporations seem likely to come to an end. It has been necessary for me to watch closely most of my life the operations of great establishments owned by hundreds of absent capitalists and conducted by salaried officers. Contrasted with these I believe that the partnership conducted by men vitally interested and owning the works will make satisfactory dividends when the corporation is embarrassed and scarcely knows upon which side the balance is to be at the end of a year's operations. The great dry goods houses that interest their most capable men in the profits of each department succeed, when those fail that endeavor to work with salaried men only. Even in the management of our great hotels, it is found wise to take into partnership the principal men.

In every branch of business this law is at work, and concerns are prosperous just in proportion as they succeed in interesting in the profits a larger and larger proportion of their ablest workers. Cooperation in this form is fast coming in all great establishments. The manufacturing business that does not have practical manufacturing partners had better supply the omission without delay, and probably the very men required are the bright young mechanics who have distinguished themselves while working for a few dollars per day or the youths from the polytechnic school. Instances constantly occur where the corporation unwilling to interest a promising practical man loses his services, and sees an interest given him by some able individual manufacturer or commercial firm who are constantly on the lookout for that indispensable article — ability.

BUILDING TO LAST

It has not hitherto been the practice for corporations properly to reward these embryo managers, but this they must come to, if they are to stand the competition of works operated by those interested in the profits.

Corporations, on the other hand, as I desire to point out to practical young men, have one advantage. Their shares are sold freely. If a worker wishes to become interested in any branch of manufacturing in America today, the path is easy. For $50 or $100 he can become a stockholder. It is becoming more and more common for workers so to invest their savings. There are many well-managed corporations whose assets and prestige enable them to earn satisfactory returns, and no better evidence of capacity and of good judgment can a workman give to his employers than that furnished by the presence of his name upon the books as a shareholder in the concern.

Workingmen have a prejudice against showing their employers that the wages they earn suffice to enable them to save, but this is a mistake. The saving workman is the valuable workman, and the wise employer regards the fact that he does save as prima facie evidence that there is something exceptionally valuable in him. It should be the effort of every corporation to induce its principal workers to invest their savings in its shares. Only in this way can corporations hope to cope successfully with individual manufacturers who have already discovered one of the valuable secrets of unusual success, viz: to share their profits with those who are most instrumental in producing them. The day of the absent capitalist stockholder, who takes no interest in the operation of the works beyond the receipt of his dividend, is certainly passing away.

The day of the valuable active worker in the industrial world is coming. Let, therefore, no young, practical workman be discouraged. On the contrary, let him be cheered. More and more, it is becoming easier for the mechanic or practical man of real ability to dictate terms to his employers. Where there was one avenue of promotion, there are now a dozen. The enormous concern of the future is to divide its profits, not among hundreds of idle capitalists who contribute nothing to its success, but among hundreds of its ablest employees, upon whose abilities and exertions success greatly depends. The capitalist absent stockholder is to be replaced by the able and present worker.

BUILDING TO LAST

As to the qualifications necessary for the promotion

of young practical men, one cannot do better than quote George Eliot, who put the matter very pithily:

"I'll tell you how I got on. I kept my ears and my eyes open, and I made my master's interest my own."

The condition precedent for promotion is, that the man must first attract notice. He must do something unusual, and especially must this be beyond the strict boundary of his duties. He must suggest, or save, or perform some service for his employer which he could not be censured for not having done. When he has thus attracted the notice of his immediate superior, whether that be only the foreman of a gang, it matters not. The first great step has been taken, for upon his immediate superior promotion depends. How high he climbs is his own affair.

We often hear men complaining that they get no chance to show their ability, and when they do show ability that it is not recognized. There is very little in this. Self-interest compels the immediate superior to give the highest place under him to the man who can best fill it, for the officer is credited with the work of his department. No man can keep another down. It will be noticed that many of the practical men who have earned fame and fortune have done so through holding on to improvements which they have made.

Improvements are easily made by practical men in the branch in which they are engaged, for they have the most intimate knowledge of the problems to be solved there. It is in this way that many of our valuable improvements have come. The man who has made an improvement should always have an eye upon obtaining an interest in the business rather than an increase of salary. Even if the business up to this time has not become very prosperous, if he has the proper stuff in him, he believes that he could make it so, and so he could. All forms of business have their ups and downs. Seasons of depression and buoyancy succeed each other, one year of great profits, several years with little or none. This is a law of the business world, into the reasons of which I need not enter. Therefore the able young practical man should not have much regard as to a choice of the branch of business.

Any business properly conducted will yield during a period of years a handsome return.

Reflection Section

How to Win Fortune

In this sweeping chapter, Carnegie examines the two main realms of labor: agricultural and industrial. He offers a spirited defense of the working man's potential to rise in either. While landownership is steadily spreading among individual farmers, industry, he observes, is concentrating on larger enterprises. Still, he argues, opportunity has not vanished, it has only changed form. The door to ownership and leadership, especially in business, still swings open for those who demonstrate exceptional ability, initiative, and loyalty.

Carnegie draws a bold contrast between college graduates and practical workers, noting that those who begin early—mechanics, clerks, and apprentices—often rise higher in business than those who enter later with academic credentials. He champions applied education, real-world experience, and the willingness to exceed expectations. Ultimately, he promotes a future in which the most capable workers become not only trusted employees but profit-sharing partners, replacing the idle absentee shareholder with the energetic and invested contributor.

Guided Reflection

1. "Make your master's interest one with your own."

Carnegie emphasizes that loyalty, initiative, and a spirit of ownership are what distinguish promotable workers.

- In your current work, how could you go beyond your official role to show leadership, care, or ingenuity?

- Whose success are you actively invested in— and who is invested in yours?

2. "There is no lion in the path."

Despite increasing industrial consolidation, Carnegie insists that ability can still rise, even in vast enterprises.

- Have you felt discouraged by the size or power of your industry?

- What steps could you take now to become indispensable or even irreplaceable where you are?

3. "The saving workman is the valuable workman."

He affirms the virtue of investing not just effort but savings into the companies one believes in.

- Do you see yourself as a stakeholder in the mission of your work—or merely an employee?

- What would it look like for you to invest more fully, whether through finances, ideas, or long-term commitment?

4. "Practical education beats pedigree."

Carnegie challenges the conventional prestige of university degrees, praising instead the hands-on learner with a spirit of initiative.

- What practical experience or skill are you currently building that will increase your value over time?

- Is there a form of training or knowledge you've been postponing that could help you grow into a leadership role?

5. "Promotion depends also on being noticed."

He notes that every great rise begins with someone doing something beyond their duty—something that gets noticed.

- Have you taken any bold or creative actions recently that revealed your potential?

- What improvement, innovation, or risk could you offer in your field that goes beyond **what's expected?**

Chapter 6

Wealth and its Uses

Wealth is the business of the world.

That the acquisition of money is the business of the world arises from the fact that, with few unfortunate exceptions, young men are born to poverty, and therefore under the salutary operation of that remarkably wise law which makes for their good: "Thou shalt earn thy bread by the sweat of thy brow."

It is the fashion nowadays to bewail poverty as an evil, to pity the young man who is not born with a silver spoon in his mouth, but I heartily subscribe to President Garfield's doctrine that "The richest heritage a young man can be born to is poverty."

I make no idle prediction when I say that is it from that class from whom the good and the great will spring. It is not from the sons of the millionaire or the noble that the world receives its teachers, its martyrs, its inventors, its statesmen, its poets, or even its men of affairs. It is from the cottage of the poor that all these spring.

We can scarcely read one among the few "immortal names that were not born to die," or who has rendered exceptional service to our race, who had not the advantage of being cradled, nursed, and reared in the stimulating school of poverty. There is nothing so enervating, nothing so deadly in its effects upon the qualities which lead to the highest achievement, moral or intellectual, as hereditary wealth.

And if there be among you a young man who feels that he is not compelled to exert himself in order to earn and live from his own efforts, I tender him my profound sympathy. Should such an one prove an exception to his fellows and become a citizen living a life creditable to himself and useful to the State, instead of my profound sympathy I bow before him with profound reverence. For one who overcomes the seductive temptations which surround hereditary wealth is of the "salt of the earth," and entitled to double honor.

It is not the poor young man who goes forth to his work in the morning and labors until evening that we should pity. It is the son of the rich man to whom

Wealth and its Uses

Providence has not been so kind as to trust with this honorable task. It is not the busy man, but the man of idleness, who should arouse our sympathy and cause us sorrow.

"Happy is the man who has found his work," says Carlyle.

I say, "Happy is the man who has to work and to work hard, and work long."

A great poet has said: "He prayeth best who loveth best."

Someday this may be parodied into: "He prayeth best who worketh best."

An honest day's work well performed is not a bad sort of prayer. The cry goes forth often nowadays, Abolish poverty! Fortunately, this cannot be done, and the poor we are always to have with us. Abolish poverty, and what would become of the race? Progress and development would cease. Consider its future if dependent upon the rich. The supply of the good and the great would cease, and human society retrograde into barbarism.

BUILDING TO LAST

Abolish luxury, if you please, but leave us the soil, upon which alone the virtues and all that is precious in human character grow: poverty — honest poverty.

I will assume for the moment that you were fortunate enough to be born poor. Then the first question that presses upon you is this: What shall I learn to do for the community which will bring me in exchange enough wealth to feed, clothe, lodge, and keep me independent of charitable aid from others? What shall I do for a living?

And the young man may like, or think that he would like, to do one thing rather than another, to pursue one branch or another, to be a businessman or craftsman of some kind, or minister, physician, electrician, architect, editor, or lawyer. I have no doubt some of you in your wildest flights aspire to be journalists. But it does not matter what the young man likes or dislikes, he always has to keep in view the main point: Can I attain such a measure of proficiency in the branch preferred as will certainly enable me to earn a livelihood by its practice ?

Wealth and its Uses

The young man, therefore, who resolves to make himself useful to his kind, and therefore entitled to receive in return from a grateful community which he benefits the sum necessary for his support, sees clearly one of the highest duties of a young man. He meets the vital question immediately pressing upon him for decision and decides it rightly.

So far, then, there is no difference about the acquisition of wealth. Everyone agrees that it is the first duty of a young person to so train himself as to be self-supporting. Nor is there difficulty about the next step, for the young person cannot be said to have performed the whole of his duty if he leaves out of account the contingencies of life, liability to accident, illness, and trade depressions like the present. Wisdom calls upon him to have regard for these things, and it is a part of his duty that he begin to save a portion of his earnings and invest them, not in speculation, but in securities or in property, or in a legitimate business in such form as will, perhaps, slowly but yet surely grow into the reserve upon which he can fall back in emergencies or in old age, and live upon his own savings.

I think we are all agreed as to the duty of laying up a competence, and hence to retain our self-respect.

BUILDING TO LAST

Besides this, I take it that some of you have already decided, just as soon as possible to ask a soon-to-be spouse to share their lot, or perhaps lots, and, of course, they should have a lot or two to share. Marriage is a very serious business indeed and gives rise to many weighty considerations.

"Be sure to marry a woman with good common-sense," was the advice given me by my mentor, and I just hand it down to you. Common sense is the most uncommon and most valuable quality in man or woman. But before you have occasion to provide yourself with a helpmate, there comes the subject upon which I am to address you — Wealth — not wealth in millions, but simply revenue sufficient for modest, independent living. This opens up the entire subject of wealth in a greater or less degree.

Now, what is wealth?

How is it created and distributed? There are not far from us immense beds of coal which have lain for millions of years useless, and therefore valueless. Through some experiment, or perhaps accident, it was discovered that black stone would burn and give forth heat. Men sank shafts, erected machinery, mined and brought forth coal, and sold it to the *community*. It displaced the use of wood as fuel, say at one-half the cost. Immediately every bed of coal became valuable because useful, or capable of being made so, and *so* a new article worth thousands of millions was added to the wealth of the community.

A Scotch mechanic one day, as the story goes, gazing into the fire upon which water was boiling in a kettle, saw the steam raise the lid, as hundreds of thousands had seen before him, but none saw in that sight what he did — the steam engine, which does the work of the world at a cost so infinitely trifling compared with what the plans known before involved, that the wealth of the world has been increased one dares not estimate how much.

The saving that the community makes is the root of wealth in any branch of material development. Now, a young man's *labor* or service to the community creates wealth just in proportion as his service is useful to the community, as it either saves or improves upon existing methods. Commodore Vanderbilt saw, I think, thirteen different short railway lines between New York and *Buffalo*, involving thirteen different managements, and a disjointed and tedious service. He consolidated them all, making one direct line, over which your Empire State Express flies fifty-one miles an hour, the fastest time in the world, and a hundred passengers patronize the lines where one did in olden days.

He rendered the community a special service, which, being followed by others, reduced the cost of bringing food from the prairies of the West to your doors to a trifling sum per ton. He produced, and is *producing every day*, untold wealth to the community by so doing, and the profit he reaped for himself was but a drop in the bucket compared with that which he showered upon the State and the nation.

Now, in the olden days, before steam, electricity, or any other of the modem inventions which unitedly have changed the whole aspect of the world, everything was done upon a small scale. There was no room for great ideas to operate upon a large scale, and thus to produce great wealth to the inventor, discoverer, originator, or executive. New inventions gave this opportunity, and many large fortunes were made by individuals. But in our *day,* we are rapidly passing this stage of development, and few large *fortunes* can now be made in any part of the world, except from one cause, the rise in the value of real estate. Manufacturing, transportation both upon the land and upon the sea, banking, insurance, have all passed into the hands of corporations composed of hundreds and in many cases thousands of shareholders.

It is so with the great manufacturing companies; so with the great steamship lines; it is so, as you know, with banks, insurance companies, and indeed with all branches of business.

It is a great mistake for young men to say to themselves, "Oh! we cannot enter into business."

If any of you have saved as much as $50 or $100, I do not know any branch of business into which you cannot plunge at once. You can get your certificate of stock and attend the meeting of stockholders, make your speeches and suggestions, quarrel with the president, and instruct the management of the affairs of the company, and have all the rights and influence of an owner. You can buy shares in anything, from newspapers to tenement-houses; but capital is so poorly paid in these days that I advise you to exercise much circumspection before you invest.

As I have said to workingmen and to ministers, college professors, artists, musicians, and physicians, and all the professional classes: Do not invest in any business concerns whatever; the risks of business are not for such as you. Buy a home for yourself first, and if you have any surplus, buy another lot or another house, or take a mortgage upon one, or upon a railway, and let it be a first mortgage, and be satisfied with moderate interest.

Do you know that out of every hundred that attempt business upon their own account, statistics are said to show that ninety-five sooner or later fail?

I know that from my own experience. I can quote the lines of Hudibras and tell you, as far as one manufacturing branch is concerned, that what he found to be true is still true to an eminent degree today:

> "Ay me! What perils do environ
> The man that meddles with cold iron!"

The shareholders of iron and steel concerns today can certify that this is so, whether the iron or steel be hot or cold; and such is also the case in other branches of business.

Wealth and its Uses

The principal complaint against our industrial conditions of today is that they cause great wealth to flow into the hands of the few. Well, of the very few, indeed, is this true. It was formerly so, as I have explained, immediately after the new inventions had changed the conditions of the world. Today it is not true. Wealth is being more and more distributed among the many. The amount of the combined profits of labor and capital which goes to labor was never so great as today, the amount going to capital never so small. While the earnings of capital have fallen more than one-half, in many cases have been entirely obliterated, statistics prove that the earnings of labor were never so high as they were previous to the recent unprecedented depression in business, while the cost of living — the necessaries of life — have fallen in some cases nearly one-half.

The question of the distribution of wealth is settling itself rapidly under present conditions and settling itself in the right direction. The few rich are getting poorer, and the toiling masses are getting richer. Nevertheless, a few exceptional men may yet make fortunes, but these will be more moderate than in the past. This may not be quite as fortunate for the masses of the people as is now believed, because great accumulations of wealth in the hands of one enterprising man who still toils on are sometimes most productive of all the forms of wealth. Take the richest man the world ever saw, who died in New York some years ago.

What was found in his case? That, with the exception of a small percentage used for daily expenses, his entire fortune and all its surplus earnings were invested in enterprises which developed the railway system of our country, which gives to the people the cheapest transportation known. Whether the millionaire wishes it or not, he cannot evade the law which under present conditions, compels him to use his millions for the good of the people. All that he gets during the few years of his life is that he may live in a finer house, surround himself with finer furniture, and works of art which may be added: he could even have a grander library, more of the gods around him. But, as far as I have known millionaires, the library is the least used part of what he would probably consider "furniture" in all his mansion. He can eat richer food and drink richer wines, which only hurt him. But truly the modem millionaire is generally a man of very simple tastes and even miserly habits.

He spends little upon himself and is the toiling bee laying up the honey in the industrial hive, which all the inmates of that hive, the community in general, will certainly enjoy. Here is the true description of the millionaire, as given by Mr. Carter in his remarkable speech before the Behring Sea tribunal at Paris:

"Those who are most successful in the acquisition of property and who acquire it to such an enormous extent are the very men who can control it, to invest it, and to handle it in the way most useful to society. It is because they have those qualities that they can engross it to so large an extent. They really own, in any just sense of the word, only what they consume. The rest is all held for the benefit of the public. They are the custodians of it. They invest it; they see that it is put into this employment, that employment, another employment. All labor is employed by it and employed in the best manner, and it is thus made the most productive. These men who acquire these hundreds of millions are really groaning under a servitude to the rest of society, for that is practically their condition, and society really endures it because it is best for them that it should be so."

Here is another estimate by a no less remarkable man. Mr. Dana, justly said at Cornell:

"That is one class of men that I refer to, the thinkers, the men of science, the inventors; and the other class is that of those whom God has endowed with a genius for saving, for getting rich, for bringing wealth together, for accumulating and concentrating money, men against whom it is now fashionable to declaim, and against whom legislation is sometimes directed. And yet is there any benefactor of humanity who is to be envied in his achievements, and in the memory and the monuments he has left behind him, more than Ezra Cornell? Or, to take another example that is here before our eyes, more than Henry W. Sage?

"These are men who knew how to get rich, because they had been endowed with that faculty; and when they got rich, they knew how to give it for great public enterprises, for uses that will remain living, immortal as long as man remains upon the earth. The men of genius and the men of money, those who prepare new agencies of life, and those who accumulate and save the money for great enterprises and great public works, these are the peculiar and the inestimable leaders of the world, as the twentieth century is opening upon us."

The bees of a hive do not destroy the honey-making bees, but the drones. It will be a great mistake for the community to shoot the millionaires, for they are the bees that make the most honey and contribute most to the hive even after they have gorged themselves full. Here is a remarkable fact, that the masses of the people in any country are prosperous and comfortable just in proportion as there are millionaires.

Take Russia, with its population little better than serfs, and living at the point of starvation upon the meanest possible fare, such fare as none of our people could or would eat, and you do not find one millionaire in Russia, always excepting the Emperor and a few nobles who own the land, owing to their political system.

It is the same, to a great extent in Germany. There are only two millionaires known to me in the whole German Empire. In France, where the people are better off than in Germany, you cannot count one half-dozen millionaires in the whole *country*. In the old home of our race, in Britain, which is the richest country in all Europe — the richest country in the world save one, our own — there are more millionaires than in the whole of the rest of Europe, and its people are better off than in any other. You come to our own land: we have more millionaires than in all the rest of the world put together, although we have not one to every ten that is reputed so. I have seen a list of supposed millionaires prepared by a well-known lawyer of Brooklyn, which made me laugh, as it has made many others. I saw men rated there as millionaires who could not pay their debts. Many should have had a cipher cut from their $1,000,000.

Some time ago I sat next to Mr. Evarts at dinner, and the conversation touched upon the idea that men should distribute their wealth during their lives for the public good. One gentleman said that was correct, giving many reasons, one of which was that, of course, they could not take it with them at death.

"Well," said Mr. Evarts, "I do not know about that. My experience as a New York lawyer is that, somehow or other, they do succeed in taking at least four-fifths of it."

Wealth and its Uses

Their reputed wealth was never found at death.

Whatever the ideal conditions may develop, it seems to me Mr. Carter and Mr. Dana are right. Under our present conditions the millionaire who toils on is the cheapest article which the community secures at the price it pays for him, namely, his shelter, clothing, and food.

The **inventions of today** lead to concentrating industrial and commercial affairs into huge concerns. You cannot work the Bessemer process successfully without employing thousands of men upon one spot. You could not make the armor for ships without first expending seven millions of dollars, as the Bethlehem Company has spent. You cannot make a yard of cotton goods in competition with the world without having an immense factory and thousands of men and women aiding in the process. The great electric establishment here in your town succeeds because it has spent millions and is prepared to do its work upon a great scale. Under such conditions it is impossible but that wealth will flow into the hands of a few men in prosperous times beyond their needs. But out of fifty great fortunes which Mr. Blaine had, he found only one man who was reputed to have made a large fortune in manufacturing.

These are made from real estate more than from all other causes combined; next follows transportation, then banking. The whole manufacturing world furnished but one millionaire.

But assuming that surplus wealth flows into the hands of a few men, **what is their duty**? How is the struggle for dollars to be lifted from the sordid atmosphere surrounding business and made a noble career?

Now, wealth has hitherto been distributed in three ways: The first and chief one is by willing it at death to the family. Now, beyond bequeathing to those dependent upon one the revenue needful for modest and independent living, is such a use of wealth either right or wise? I ask you to think over the result, as a rule, of millions given over to young men and women, the sons and daughters of the millionaire. You will find that, as a rule, it is not good for the daughters; and this is seen in the character and conduct of the men who marry them. As for the sons, you have their condition as described in the extract which I read you from The

Sun. Nothing is truer than this, that as a rule the "almighty dollar" bequeathed to sons or daughters by millions proves an almighty curse. It is not the good of the child which the millionaire parent considers when he makes these bequests, it is his own vanity; it is not affection for the child, it is self-glorification for the parent which is at the root of this injurious disposition of wealth.

There is a second use of wealth, less common than the first, which is not so injurious to the community, but which should bring no credit to the testator.

Money is left by millionaires to public institutions when they must relax their grasp upon it. There is no grace, and can be no blessing, in giving what cannot be withheld. It is no gift, because it is not cheerfully given, but only granted at the stem summons of death. The miscarriage of these bequests, the litigation connected with them, and the manner in which they are frittered away seem to prove that the Fates do not regard them with a kindly eye. We are never without a lesson that the only mode of producing lasting good by giving large sums of money is for the millionaire to give as close attention to its distribution during his *life* as he did to its acquisition.

We have today the noted case of five or six millions of dollars left by a great lawyer to found a public library in New York, an institution needed so greatly that the failure of this bequest is a misfortune. It is years since he died. The will is pronounced invalid through a flaw, although there is no doubt of the intention of the donor. It is sad commentary upon the folly of men holding the millions which they cannot use until they are unable to put them to the end they desire. Peter Cooper, Pratt of Baltimore, and Pratt of Brooklyn, and others are the type of men who should be taken by you as your model: They distributed their surplus during life.

The **third use**, and the only noble use of surplus wealth, is this: That it be regarded as a sacred trust, to be administered by its possessor, into whose hands it flows, for the highest good of the people. Man does not live by bread alone, and five or ten cents a day more revenue scattered over thousands would produce little or no good. Accumulated into a great fund and expended as Mr. Cooper expended it for the Cooper Institute, it establishes something that will last for generations. It will educate the brain, the spiritual part of man. It furnishes a ladder upon which the aspiring poor may climb; and there is no use whatever, gentlemen, trying to help people who do not help themselves. You cannot push anyone up a ladder unless he be willing to climb a little himself. When you stop boosting, he falls to his injury.

Therefore, I have often said, and I now repeat, that the day is coming, and already we see its dawn, in which the man who dies possessed of millions of available wealth which was free and in his hands ready to be distributed will die disgraced. Of course I do not mean that the man in business may not be stricken down with his capital in the business, which cannot be withdrawn, for capital is the tool with which he works his wonders and produces more wealth. I refer to the man who dies possessed of millions of securities which are held simply for the interest they produce, that he may add to his hoard of miserable dollars. By administering surplus wealth during life great wealth may become a blessing to the community, and the occupation of the business man accumulating wealth may be elevated so as to rank with any profession.

BUILDING TO LAST

In this way he may take rank even with the physician, one of the highest of our professions, because he too, in a sense, will be a physician, looking after and trying not to cure, but to prevent, the ills of humanity. To those of you who are compelled or who desire to follow a business life and to accumulate wealth, I commend this idea. The epitaph which every rich man should wish himself justly entitled to is that seen upon the monument to Pitt, today:

> He lived without ostentation,
> And he died poor.

Such is the man whom the future is to *honor*, while he who dies in old age retired from business, possessed of millions of available wealth, is to die unwept, un-honored, and unsung.

I may justly **divide young men into four classes**:

First, those who must work for a living, and set before them as their aim the acquisition of a modest competence — of course, with a modest but picturesque cottage in the country and one as a companion "who maketh *sunshine* in a shady place" and is the good angel of his life. The motto of this class might be given as "Give me neither poverty nor riches." *and,* "From the anxieties of poverty as from the responsibilities of wealth, good Lord, deliver us."

Second, comprising those among you who are determined to acquire wealth, whose aim in life is to belong to that much-talked-of and grandly abused class, the millionaires, those who start to *labor* for the greatest good of the greatest number, but the greatest number always number one, the motto of this class being short and to the point: "Put money in thy purse."

Third. The god these worship is neither wealth nor happiness. They are inflamed with "noble ambition;" the desire of fame is the controlling element of their lives. Now, while this is not so ignoble as the desire for material wealth, it must be said that it betrays more vanity. The shrine of fame has many worshippers. The element of vanity is seen in its fiercest phase among those who come before the public.

It is well known, for instance, that musicians, actors, and even painters — all the artistic class — are peculiarly prone to excessive personal vanity. This has often been wondered at, but the reason probably is that the musician and the actor, and even the painter, may be transcendent in his special line without being even highly educated, without having an all-around brain. Some peculiarities, some one element in his character, may give him prominence or fame, so that his love of art, or of use through art, is entirely drowned by a narrow, selfish, personal vanity. But we find this liability in a lesser degree all through the professions, the politician, the lawyer, and, with reverence be it spoken, sometimes the minister. *Less*, I think, in the physician than in any of the professions, probably because he, more than in any other profession, is called to deal with the sad realities of life face to face. He of all men sees the vanity of vanities.

An illustration of this class is we*ll* drawn in Hotspur's address:

"By heavens, methinks it were an easy leap, To pluck bright honour from the pale-faced moon; Or dive into the bottom of the deep, Where fathom-line could never touch the ground. And pluck up drowned honour by the locks; So he that doth redeem her thence might wear Without corrival all her dignities."

Wealth and its Uses

*H*e cares not for use; he cares not for state; he cares only for himself, and, as a vain peacock, struts across the stage. *I*t does not seem to me that the love of wealth is the controlling desire of so many as the love of fame, and this is matter for sincere congratulation, and proves that under the irresistible laws of evolution the race is slowly moving onward and upward.

Take the whole range of the artistic world, which gives sweetness and light to life, which refines and adorns, and surely the great composer, painter, pianist, lawyer, judge, statesman, all those in public life, care less for millions than for professional reputation in their respective fields of *labor*. What cared Washington, Franklin, Lincoln, or Grant and Sherman for wealth? Nothing! What cared Harrison or Cleveland, two poor men, not unworthy successors? What care the Judges of our Supreme Court, or even the leading counsel that plead before them? The great preachers, physicians, great teachers, are not concerned about the acquisition of wealth. The treasure they seek is in the reputation acquired through their service to others, and this is certainly a great step from the *millionaire* class, who struggle to old age, and through old age to the verge of the grave, with no ambition, apparently, except to add to their pile of miserable dollars.

But there is a **fourth class**, higher than all the preceding, who worship neither at the shrine of wealth nor fame, but at the noblest of all shrines, the shrine of service — service to the race. Self-abnegation is its watchword. Members of this inner and higher circle seek not popular applause, are concerned not with being popular, but with being right. They say with Confucius: "It concerns me not that I have not high office; what concerns me is to make myself worthy of office."

It is not cast down by poverty, neither unduly elated by prosperity. The man belonging to this class simply seeks to do his duty day by day in such manner as may enable him to *honor* himself, fearing nothing but his own self-reproach. I have known men and women not prominently before the public, for this class courts not prominence, but who in their lives proved themselves to have reached this ideal stage. Now, I will give *you* the fitting illustration from the words of a Scotch poet who died altogether too young:

I will go forth 'mong men, not mailed in scorn.

Wealth and its Uses

But in the armour of a pure intent.

Great duties are before me, and great songs;

And whether crowned or crownless when I fall.

It matters not, so as God's work is done.

I've learned to prize the quiet lightning deed,

Not the applauding thunder at its heels

Which men call fame.

Then, standing upon the threshold of life, you have the good, better, best presented to you — the three stages of development, the natural, spiritual, and celestial, they may fitly be called. One has success in material things for its aim— not without benefit for the race as a whole, because it lifts the individual from the animal and demands the exercise of many valuable qualities: sobriety, industry, and *self-discipline*.

The second rises still higher: the reward sought for being things more of the spirit — not gross and material, but invisible, and not of the flesh, but of the brain, the spiritual part of man, and this brings into play *innumerable* virtues which make good and useful men.

The third or celestial class stands upon an entirely different footing from the others in this, that selfish considerations are subordinated in the select brotherhood of the best, the service to be done for others being the first consideration. The reward of either wealth or fame is unsought, for these have learned and know full well that virtue is its own and the only exceeding great reward, and this once enjoyed, all other rewards are not worth seeking. And so wealth and even fame are dethroned ; and there stands enthroned the highest standard of all — your own approval flowing from a faithful discharge of duty as you see it, fearing no consequences, seeking no reward.

It does not matter much what branch of effort your tastes or judgment draw you to, the one great point is that you should be drawn to some one branch.

Then perform your whole duty in it... and a little more – the "little more" being vastly important. We have the words of a great poet for it, that the man who does the best he can, can whiles do more. Maintain your self-respect as the most precious jewel of all and the only true way to win the respect of others, and then remember what Emerson says, for what he says here is true:

"No young man can be cheated out of an *honorable* career in life unless he cheat himself."

Reflection Section

Wealth and its Uses

In this final chapter, Andrew Carnegie delivers a sweeping moral and practical philosophy of wealth. He begins by reframing poverty—not as a curse but as a *blessing*—the crucible in which resilience, self-discipline, and greatness are forged. Wealth, he argues, is a tool, not a trophy. It is something to be earned through service and preserved through discipline, **but most importantly, it is to be used.** Surplus wealth, in his view, must be stewarded as a sacred trust, with the goal of uplifting others—not hoarded or passed idly to descendants.

Carnegie urges readers to resist both vanity and greed and to aspire instead toward a life of meaningful service. He outlines a hierarchy of ambition: the pursuit of self-sufficiency, then of wealth, then of fame, and finally—at the highest level—of selfless contribution. In doing so, he invites us not just to build fortune, but to *build character*.

Wealth and its Uses

1. "Happy is the man who has to work."
Carnegie celebrates labor as a noble calling, not a burden.

- How has hard work shaped your character, habits, or worldview?

- Do you view your work as merely a necessity—or something with potential to refine you?

2. "Wealth is a sacred trust."

He insists that surplus wealth should be actively administered for public good, not stockpiled or left behind in a will.

- If you consider your resources—money, time, knowledge—which of these might be put to use for the benefit of others right now?

- Are there causes, communities, or people who could flourish with your help?

3. "The best use of wealth is to lift others."

Carnegie admires those who establish ladders for others to climb.

- What ladder have you already built for someone else—formally or informally?

- What would it look like to create something (a scholarship, a journal, a mentorship, a business) that outlasts you?

4. "Virtue is the only exceeding great reward."

He classifies ambition into three forms: for wealth, for fame, and for service—and urges us to seek the last.

- Where would you place your current goals on Carnegie's hierarchy?

- What small shift could move you closer to a life of service rather than a life of self-seeking?

5. "No young man can be cheated... unless he cheat himself."

Carnegie ends on a call to personal responsibility.

- Where in your life are you currently undercutting your own potential?

- What would it mean to live today in full alignment with your values, regardless of outcome?

AVAILABLE FROM CHOICE PRESS

The Choice Legacy Collection

Alone in the Fire   **Passing Down The Legacy Journal**

Available now at **choice-press.com**

Interested in writing your own Legacy memoir?

Reach out to us at
editorial@choice-press.com